Divorce and the Bible

A systematic exegesis to challenge the traditional views

Colin Hamer

Bloomington, IN   Milton Keynes, UK
authorHOUSE

AuthorHouse™
1663 Liberty Drive, Suite 200
Bloomington, IN 47403
www.authorhouse.com
Phone: 1-800-839-8640

AuthorHouse™ UK Ltd.
500 Avebury Boulevard
Central Milton Keynes, MK9 2BE
www.authorhouse.co.uk
Phone: 08001974150

© *2006 Colin Hamer. All rights reserved.*

No part of this book may be reproduced, stored in a retrieval system, or transmitted by any means without the written permission of the author.

First published by AuthorHouse 11/6/2006

ISBN: 1-4259-3355-6 (e)
ISBN: 1-4259-0750-4 (sc)

Printed in the United States of America
Bloomington, Indiana

This book is printed on acid-free paper.

All Bible quotations are taken from New International Version (NIV) unless otherwise stated

For Trevor Baker

Without whose stimulating conversations this book would never have been written

The composition of this book has been for the author a long struggle of escape, and so must the reading of it be for most readers if the author's assault upon them is to be successful, - a struggle of escape from habitual modes of thought and expression......
The difficulty lies, not in the new ideas, but in escaping from the old ones, which ramify, for those brought up as most of those have been, into every corner of our minds.

John Maynard Keynes, from his preface to 'The General Theory of Employment, Interest and Money' 1935

Acknowledgements

I would like to thank all the friends who, as I worked on this book, not only bore with me, but encouraged me on the way. I particularly mention Cynthia – twice divorced but loved by God.

Table of Contents

Preface xiii
Introduction xvii
1 Marriage – a Covenant 1
2 Marriage – a One Flesh Union 11
3 The Traditional Views 25
4 The Thesis 27
5 The Old Testament and Divorce 34
6 Jesus and Divorce 50
7 Paul and Divorce 76
8 Remarriage after Divorce 91
9 Various Objections Considered 101
10 A Practical Outworking 106
11 The Key Points 114
12 A Conclusion 117
Appendix 1: Deuteronomy 24 123
Appendix 2: The Levitical Death Penalty ... 127
Appendix 3: Mark 10:12 131
Appendix 4: Adultery 139
Appendix 5: Agunah 151

Preface

The secular Western world is having problems with marriage; while still seen as an ideal, the number of divorces in the UK is currently running at just over half the number of marriages contracted in recent years.[1] Further, cohabitation has become a norm. We have come to accept that the girl next door, and the heir to the throne, will sleep with their partners without a marriage certificate.

The Christian church meanwhile seems embattled in its own teaching. The Church of Rome holds the line that there must be an official Church marriage and then no divorce, but finds grounds for declaring some marriages to be null, thus permitting the couple remarriage to different partners. In turn the Church of England and non-conformist churches by and large hold that marriages should be at least registered by the state and that the core teachings of the Reformation about divorce still stand.

Many books have been written on divorce, but really there are only four or five books written several times over, as they all tend to rehearse one of the views outlined in Chapter 3, the denominational background of the author often determining which model he takes as his starting point. But the Bible does not fit well with the divorce teachings expounded in the commentaries today. The number of fundamental contradictions between their expositions is often startling.

There are however four areas that nearly all agree on:-

1. A wife in Old Testament times could not divorce her husband
2. A husband in both Testaments could divorce his wife for her sexual impurity
3. Jesus teaches that a wife can [only] divorce her husband for his sexual impurity
4. The New Testament teaches that the guilty party in a divorce based on sexual misconduct cannot remarry

---

[1] National Statistics Census 2001. Figures based on year 2000

The first point is factually incorrect, the third and fourth points are not found in the New Testament, or indeed anywhere in the Bible.

Our view of the Bible's teaching about marriage and divorce has the potential to impact so greatly on our daily and church lives, so why is there such confusion and compromise in this vitally important area? One reason is that divorce is dealt with only briefly in the New Testament. In the gospels only thirteen words are spoken about divorce from a wife's perspective.[2] To get a fuller picture it is necessary to look elsewhere in the Bible and then make some assumptions; it is these assumptions that have led to most of the debate and disagreements on divorce within the Christian community.

It is critical in formulating a biblical position on divorce that the assumptions are biblically based. This is often not the case. One example will suffice; all the Christian literature on divorce I have surveyed relies on the Western secular humanist assumption that gender equality means gender 'sameness'. That assumption is then used as a basis for interpreting the divorce passages in the New Testament. In other words it is assumed the rules and guidelines on divorce must be the same for husbands and wives. It is with this mindset that the subject is approached.

Commentators, even when they claim not to come to marriage with an androgynous mindset, do so when they come to divorce.[3] All the current views widely held in the Christian church rely on the assumption that the New Testament removes all gender distinctions in divorce.

It is this assumption, and other secular ideas that have permeated the church's teaching about marriage, that have caused our perspective on the Bible's teaching about divorce to be compromised. Marriage is seen as being primarily about children, mutual support and personal fulfilment, and the marriage bond being primarily about sexual intimacy. Grounds for divorce outlined in most Christian books on the

---

[2] Mark 10:12 New International Version
[3] For example 'God, Marriage and Family' Andreas Kostenberger. Crossway 2004 p37

subject are based solely on the failure of integrity in that sexual intimacy.

Shocking as it might seem to the modern Western mind (secular and Christian) its own view of marriage (and divorce) is often not the thrust of the Bible's teaching. The Bible teaches that marriage is primarily a picture of Christ's relationship with his redeemed church - thus roles in marriage are gender specific. Grounds for divorce are based on the breach of those gender specific roles, when the picture of Christ and the church is spoiled.

The individual verses of the Bible that speak of divorce might be considered as pieces of a jigsaw. The divorce views widely held today were first promulgated in the Reformation; the Reformers realised that their arrangement of the jigsaw pieces did not fit together well, and what was worse - there was a piece missing! They could find no grounds for divorce for a wife. The solution? Make a new piece for the one not found in the box – namely a wife's [only] grounds for divorce is her husband's sexual unfaithfulness – and 'press' that in. Nobody it seems had thought to look at the picture on the front of the box; with the Bible's picture of Christ and the church, rather than pragmatism or secular rationalism, new insights could have been gained and 'difficult' Scriptures would have fallen into place.

Our Western world is hugely indebted (often unwittingly) to these great teachers of the Reformation, but surely it is the task of any believer not to defend any particular body of doctrine, but to be always reforming, always going back to Scripture, to see new wonders and riches of grace there.[4] I hope my readers will be like the Bereans Paul speaks of in Acts 17, and see if what is being said in this thesis is actually what is taught in the Bible.

---

[4] Actually the views on divorce held widely by the evangelical community were first expounded by the humanist Erasmus (1466-1536)

Introduction

Why did God make Adam? If God is perfect, complete, all knowing, all wise – why did he want Adam, and furthermore want a relationship with him? Whatever the answer to this, the Bible tells us God did indeed make the first man, and in turn gave him a desire for a relationship with his creator. So it is that in all cultures and peoples the quest to find God and worship him is witnessed in many kinds of religious rituals and beliefs. But without another human to relate to Adam was perceived to be incomplete – so God made Eve.

All this we read in the first chapters of the Old Testament. There are many 'givens' in the Bible and we have to accept that this aspect of the Godhead, a desire for relationships, he wove into our human nature. The most fundamental of those relationships is between a man and a woman, a husband and wife. God brought Adam and Eve together, to be committed to each other for life.

These Edenic beginnings however concealed a much deeper purpose for marriage, a purpose progressively revealed as Scripture unfolded. The Old and New Testaments are consistent, that although marriage is about love, companionship, and children, it is above all a picture of God's relationship with his people, a relationship that will come to full fruition at the consummation of history in the wedding supper of the Lamb.

But first came the 'Fall'; sin came into the world and spoiled the relationship between man and God, and between man and woman. In a sense the rest of the Bible story, and our human story, is about damaged relationships. Not that everything is wrong; harmony and beauty remain – but we see much in our world that is not as it should be.

This includes marriage. Marital disharmony has existed since that first fall from favour, but the steep increase in the number of divorces in recent years, particularly in the West, reveals its extent. The church has not been immune from this; many congregations now have members who have been divorced, church leaders struggling to combine consistent biblical teaching with a compassionate approach. While the breakdown of a marriage relationship is always a result of sinful behaviour, the Bible teaches that divorce itself is not necessarily wrong; some might use divorce sinfully but God allows for divorce without sin – indeed the Bible tells us that our holy God divorced Israel. [5] But every passage where divorce is spoken of teaches the same thing; marriage is an earthly picture of the relationship between God and his people – divorce is allowed when either spouse spoils that picture.

However the Roman Catholic Church (and some others) has a sacramental view of marriage. This view teaches that when a couple are married on earth something happens in heaven and as a consequence the union is indissoluble. Such people either think that any divorce is sinful, or that there is no divorce at all and so any subsequent relationship is adulterous.

Since the Reformation, in most churches, husbands have been allowed to divorce their wives for sexual unfaithfulness, based on the clear teaching of Matthew 5 and 19. Wives have been allowed to divorce their husbands for sexual unfaithfulness, based on a doctrine squeezed into Mark 10:12, even though in that verse no such grounds are given. The rationale? A husband's adultery would have meant his death in the Old Testament economy, so freeing his wife from the marriage; and secondly, in the New Testament economy, it is considered only fair to allow for wives what is allowed for husbands. The main thrust of this thesis shows that this rationale is fatally flawed both exegetically and theologically. (The two arguments used in the rationale are considered in more detail in Appendix 2 and Appendix 3 respectively).

It will be seen that the Old Testament, in teaching and practice, allowed a wife to divorce her husband for his failure to provide for her materially and emotionally, but restricted the husband's right to divorce to that of sexual impurity by his wife.

In the New Testament Jesus clarified that it really was for sexual impurity alone that a man can divorce his wife – much to the dismay of his disciples. There is no

---

[5] Jeremiah 3:8

record of him discussing the wife's grounds for divorce, but the apostle Paul applied the Old Testament principle about wives, teaching that desertion is just cause for a wife to divorce her husband.

Some definitions

Christians often equate 'marriage' and 'divorce' to the secular state's position on these matters - the state registration of a marriage or a divorce is used to determine the status of the couple. This has practical difficulties, and is not a biblical concept.

If I can illustrate by way of two personal anecdotes. I know of two couples cohabiting for more than 10 years but one partner in each relationship is actually married to the partner in the other relationship – they had never dissolved their original failed marriages. Who in God's eyes are they married to?

Recently my uncle announced that he was marrying a woman called Linda. This was of some surprise to us because he had been married to a Linda for 25 years and they had two adult children. He went on to inform us that it was the same Linda – but they had never actually registered the relationship with the state – she had simply changed her name to that of my Uncle's. Were they already married in God's eyes?

A definition of Christian marriage will be attempted in Chapters 1 and 2, but any committed heterosexual relationship should surely be approached prime face as if it is a marriage, and any counselling given to the couple if they wanted to split up be undertaken on that basis. Only if the relationship was not biblically valid, for example if it was homosexual, incestuous, or not consensual, should the couple be treated as if they were not married.

Problems of exegesis

Jesus only spoke about divorce briefly in the gospels and in the rest of the New Testament there is really only one passage – 1 Corinthians 7. In light of this it is important to know the background to the New Testament narrative

- perhaps more so than with any other doctrinal issue impacting the church today.

Care needs to be taken that we do not import into our interpretation secular principles and assumptions that we are so familiar with that we often have difficulty in realising that we are using them as our terms of reference - principles and assumptions that would not be in the minds of first century Christians.

Nowhere is this more pronounced than in the matter of gender distinctives. Secular humanism of the 21st century has largely equated gender equality with sameness. It says that men and women are perfectly suited to any role. Any differences that are accepted, exist only in the area of sexual reproduction, or are believed to be culturally conditioned. This thinking is then often applied to marriage and divorce. No matter how reasonable this seems to us it is a framework of reference that is not found in the Bible. The Bible teaches that gender does matter in the church, in marriage, and in divorce.

It is impossible to explore every doctrinal position thoroughly ourselves. We rely on those more mature spiritually, for example our pastor, our elders, our denomination, to have worked out a biblical position on those matters we have not investigated ourselves. It can be unsettling to find that the divorce view we have been taught is not well founded. The natural reaction is to defend our position against any new teaching, not because we have thought it through carefully, but because we want to be loyal to those we have trusted in this matter. A further problem is many of us have had close friends and/or family who have divorced. There are personal traumas and lasting hurts. It is difficult to be completely dispassionate or neutral on these matters.

Principles of exegesis to be used

To make a fair attempt at looking at the biblical teaching these five 'rules' will be adopted:-

1. No verse or statement on its own, referring to divorce or remarriage, will be considered to be the whole

teaching about the subject

2. Where a verse is unclear parts of Scripture that are more clear will be used as an aid in interpretation

3. Some statements recorded in the Bible might have implied thoughts in them that can be established because they are clearly stated elsewhere in Scripture, or with some caution, be reasonably assumed were in the mind of the hearers

4. Where the New Testament is silent it will not be automatically assumed that the relevant Old Testament teaching can no longer be used as a guide

5. Something will not be ruled 'out' or 'in' simply because the early church fathers, leaders of the Reformation, or my church, does or does not teach it - or our society does or does not approve of it

Further - the Bible is clear that marriage is an earthly picture of the church's redemption by Christ.[6] The Old Testament often portrays God as the husband and (a largely faithless) Israel as his wife. In the New Testament the wife is a picture of the church and the husband a picture of Christ.

While not forcing this or pressing details too greatly, it will form part of the exegesis. When a passage about divorce seems unclear, or even illogical, the spiritual truth signified (Christ and the church) will be looked at to see what the Bible might be saying about the sign (earthly marriage) – and use that as an aid in understanding what the passage is saying.

---

[6] 'Church' of course has several meanings in common use: a local fellowship, a denomination, or even a building, as well as its 'true' meaning of all those redeemed in Christ, past, present and future. I hope the context will make clear its use in this thesis.

> **Key Points**
>
> - **Five 'rules' of exegesis will be used**
>
> - **Marriage is an earthly picture of a believer's redemption in Christ and this can further help us to understand the biblical basis for divorce**

1 Marriage – a Covenant

What is marriage?

Marriage was designed for us, for our benefit. Eve was given to Adam because without her God perceived that he was alone.[7] Eve was created as a companion for Adam, a life - and lifelong partner.[8] Under its protection children could be brought into the world and nurtured.[9] These aspects of marriage – mutual loving support and the raising of children in a family environment - are the stuff of films, novels, advice books and much Christian literature. They dominate our thought processes whenever we think of the subject. Any word association test of 'marriage' would show the pre-eminence of them.

And of course all this is not wrong, but none of these truths define marriage. The emphasis on these things in much of the literature on marriage, both Christian and secular, has obscured an important truth; love is love - but marriage is a contract - a lifelong contract between a man and a woman.[10] No matter how unromantic this might sound when a couple marry they are entering into mutual obligations. And specifically the contractual relationship between a man and wife is to reflect the contract that God has with his people. The Bible word for this contract is more usually called a covenant. [11]

---

[7] Genesis 2:18
[8] Matthew 19:5,6
[9] Genesis 1:28
[10] Marriage is exclusively heterosexual in the Bible. There are no same sex marriages.
[11] Kostenberger 'God Marriage and Family' Crossway 2004 has an interesting section (p83ff) where he compares and contrasts a contract with a covenant. Marriage is not entirely like a private contract in that it is done before God; but neither is it exactly like the covenant God has with us, as God imposed the terms of the covenant on his people. The marriage contract symbolises the heavenly covenant without it being an exact equivalent. See also Instone-Brewer 'Divorce and Remarriage in the Bible' Eerdmans 2002 p 15-19

The heavenly covenant

The Bible uses the term covenant or testament to describe the relationship God had with his people Israel; he would be their God, they would be his people. There were mutual obligations; he would provide and care, they were to honour and obey. Then Jesus revealed the terms of the new covenant, the New Testament, where we see the full outworking of grace. Jesus would take to heaven all those that loved and trusted him, regardless of all the old rule keeping. For those with eyes to see, the new covenant was in fact embedded in the old. Jesus promised to provide and care for his church – all those that believe on him – and in turn we are to honour and obey him.

The Bible repeatedly compares these covenants with the marriage covenant, describing God as the bridegroom to Old Testament Israel, Jesus the bridegroom to his church. [12] The outworking of an earthly marriage is to be a visual aid to illustrate the great rescue operation mounted by God the Father, effected by God the Son, and secured in our hearts by God the Holy Spirit.

The covenantal roles are gender based

The mutual obligations of marriage are clearly laid out by specific mention and repeated example in the Bible – being determined by our gender. Marriage in its covenant outworking is to serve as a picture of Christ and his relationship to his church, where the husband symbolises Christ and his wife the church. Marriage is an earthly contract to mirror a heavenly reality.

Humans were created *male and female*. This was God's idea, his specific intent. Furthermore, the Bible says that *in the image of God he created him; male and female he created them.*[13] In some mysterious way, Adam and Eve together are a reflection of God himself; our human sexuality has its origins in the nature of the Godhead. Our maleness and femaleness is not an aberration — a function

---

[12] For example Jeremiah 2 Revelation 21
[13] Genesis 1:27

of reproduction, a 'spin' on our true selves imposed by our culture. Rather, it reflects the nature of God as a moral and rational Being and is designed to fulfil God's purposes in the world he has created. It is from this exalted perspective that a Christian must approach the subject of gender roles.

❏ **For the husband**

For the husband we see that he is expected to exercise leadership, authority and responsibility. Right at the beginning of the human story we see that God made Adam first, gave instructions to him and asked him to account for his own and Eve's actions. [14]

As the Old Testament unfolds we see men taking the lead, often by divine appointment, in the nation's family, religious and political life. These men demonstrated every human frailty; at the Fall from that first idyllic state, during and after the destruction of the world by flood, and throughout the ups and downs of Israel's turbulent story. Despite this it was still men God chose to take the lead.

We see the same in the New Testament. Men were appointed as apostles and elders in the early church. Jesus Christ himself took on manhood at the incarnation – not womanhood. This was God's choice. His masculinity was not an arbitrary choice. To take the lead and the responsibility for redeeming the church, and the exercise of authority over it – God chose masculinity.

Early in the Pentateuch we see that a husband was to provide *food, clothing and marital rights* [15] for his wife. In the New Testament a husband's responsibility is described as loving, feeding and caring for his wife.[16] By repeated example in the Bible story the husband was ultimately responsible for providing for his wife and any children.

---

[14] Genesis 3:8-11
[15] Exodus 21:10
[16] Ephesians 5: 25-33

Divorce and the Bible

❑ **For the wife**

Eve was co-equal with Adam in creation. Together they were to literally rule the world:

God blessed them and said to them, "Be fruitful and increase in number; fill the earth and subdue it. Rule over the fish of the sea and the birds of the air and over every living creature that moves on the ground." [17]

Equality of status does not mean in this case that they had the same roles. In fact it does not necessarily mean that in any sphere of life. We are used to playing roles in life. I can be husband, father, son, employee, brother, friend and so on — all in the same day! We are all familiar with having to wear different 'hats' in different situations. So at home Susan Jones is a wife, mother, friend, neighbour and so on — but then she goes to her employment – where she is an office manager. In that role she has authority, not as Susan Jones but as a line manager appointed by her company. Her authority in that post is real, but limited to that role. She cannot go home and tell her neighbour to cut his lawn.

We see Eve created as a 'helper' to Adam. [18] We should not be put off by that word and its modern connotation of inferiority; we need to remember that in the Old Testament God himself is described as a 'helper' — the helper of Israel,[19] the helper of the fatherless [20] and the helper of David.[21] Eve's role was to support Adam in their joint custody of creation. She was, and is, in a sense, deputy chief executive of the newly created world.

There is no biblical restriction to the role of a woman in any matter to do with the affairs of this world – be it politics, business, the professions or whatever. Even in the New Testament era we have the example of Lydia as the

---

[17] Genesis 1:28
[18] Genesis 2:20
[19] Deuteronomy 33:29
[20] Psalm 10:14
[21] Psalm 27:9

seemingly independent business woman.[22] But in the home it is God's specific will that a wife accepts her husband's leadership.

Gender matters in biblical marriage

So in the home the Bible teaches that gender presupposes different roles, different responsibilities and duties for the husband and wife. If marriage is understood as a contract, what is contracted should be based on those roles. This is clearly seen in everyday life, where any contract involves more than one party, each party usually having different responsibilities and duties. For example if you enter a contract with a builder to build an extension to your home – he builds the extension and you pay the money. If you both tried to build the extension and nobody paid – or you both tried to pay but nobody did the building – it would be fruitless. Virtually all legal agreements involve the relevant parties performing different roles, fulfilling different duties. The strength of most organisations (a family is an organisation of sorts) is based on the fact that people play different roles within them. So a company might have a finance, sales and production director. It would be an unusual company that had three finance directors and none of the other posts represented.

Gender role confusion today

Confusion has arisen because the trend today is to blur the roles in marriage, many church services talking of equal partnerships where the sub-text is that each has the same role. Indeed the Church of England has the bride and groom make each promise to the other exactly the same things;[23] how can this reflect the divine theme of Christ and the church spoken of in the same service?

    The concept of defined roles in marriage has been largely lost in contemporary society; politicians, the media and the church all tell us that husbands and wives are

---

[22] Acts 16:4
[23] Alternative Service Book 1980 (as amended in 2000)

equal partners. Strangely this has not always been followed through in the [UK] legal system, either in the divorce courts or in the Child Support Agency, where the needs of wives and children seem to predominate. [24]

No covenant – no marriage?

Not only is there confusion about roles within conventional marriage, many couples choose not to make any formal agreement between themselves, perhaps not even discussing role expectations. Is such cohabitation marriage?

Is marriage:

- Any heterosexual couple in a sexual relationship?
- Any heterosexual couple in a 'committed' sexual relationship?
- Any heterosexual relationship that has been sanctioned by a recognised church?
- Any heterosexual relationship registered with the state?

At the time of writing it is probably true that for the majority of Christians it is only the last relationship listed that would qualify as a marriage. This is a strangely inconsistent position for the Christian church to take. They would not accept the state's jurisdiction on who they define as a Christian, who is to be baptised, or who is to take communion – so why let the state have the final say on what constitutes marriage? If state registration of the relationship is the litmus test of marriage, none of the man and wife couples named in Genesis, for example, could be considered to be properly 'married', as there was no concept of a modern state at

---

[24] *'divorce settlements used to be* [up until year 2000 White v White] *calculated using an amalgam of considerations such as age expectations, earning capacity and reasonable needs of the wife (though not the husband).* ' Sandra Davis of prominent divorce solicitors Mishcon de Reya quoted from The Investor issue 45 2005 p10

Marriage – a Covenant

that time. [25] This is an important question as an increasing number of couples do not register their relationship with the state or formalise it with any religious ceremony – indeed it is possible civil marriage as a state institution will not last. [26] If a church assumes that any cohabiting couple whose relationship is not state registered, or who have made no formal or public commitment, are not married, does this mean if such a relationship fails that 'divorce' counselling is superfluous? That neither partner in such a relationship has any duty to the other that is rooted in biblical teaching? This is similar to the confusion that both the church and the world often demonstrate over baptism – confusing the sign with the thing signified. You can be a Christian without baptism – and conversely evangelicals consider that baptism never saved anybody. Surely you can be 'married' without any of the trappings of a traditional marriage. And cohabitation is not just a phenomena among young people. There are couples in their seventies who have cohabited for decades – even having grandchildren. Can we go to them with an open Bible and say they must repent of this? Certainly the Bible commends a public and formal commitment, and I would personally strongly recommend it – but it is not a command of Scripture. It might be quite legitimate for church leaders to insist on couples who are church members having a formal ceremony; however I do not believe Christians should be telling their unbelieving

---

[25] Indeed civil marriage legislation only came to England in 1857. Before that marriage was regulated by the church.

[26] Civil Partnership legislation came into force in the UK on 5 December 2005. The government is at the time of writing being sued by two British lesbians who had their 'marriage' solemnised in Canada and want it recognised in the UK, rejecting the civil partnership status as not being an equivalent. By its very nature civil marriage discriminates on the basis of gender orientation and surely the government will face further challenges on this – challenges which at a stroke could be removed by dropping civil marriage altogether. The Registrar General's Office has already stated that there will be moves to 'make things consistent' between civil marriages and civil partnerships (Daily Telegraph 1 August 2005). In any case the number of state registered marriages is in steep decline. (See Population Trends Published by UK Government September 2005)

neighbours that they are actively living in sin because they have not gone through such a ceremony.

But certainly Jesus stated that it was God's intention that a man and wife were to be so for life. The sexual act itself (as shall be seen in the next chapter) does not itself constitute marriage; what is required in addition is some sort of covenant, or at least if we accept the above analysis an intention, that presupposes the relationship to be a permanent one. Surely where there is such an 'intention of permanence' the relationship should be considered a marriage. [27]

From a biblical perspective then:

Marriage is a heterosexual couple choosing to go through life together with a covenant of permanence (even if only implied), consummated with sexual intercourse.

But their relationship might not reflect the Bible's teaching; so while it is possible to counsel such a couple about divorce using biblical guidelines they would not necessarily feel bound by them. In contrast the Bible is clear - a Christian marriage is when a man agrees to provide emotionally and financially for a woman for the rest of her life (to the best of his ability), and for the woman to accept this man's headship. There is to be a promise of mutual care and consideration and the relationship be consummated sexually. The husband is to be like Christ to his wife, nurturing her and caring for her. The wife is to receive from her husband, in metaphor, the sustenance that the church receives from Christ. She is to be faithful to her husband as the church is to be to her Lord.

---

[27] A view Cornes takes see 'Divorce and Remarriage' Eerdmans 1993 p43. In Scotland until 1940 a couple could be married by simply expressing mutual consent in the presence of any two witnesses. See Cornes 'Divorce and Remarriage' Eerdmans 1993 p42

Marriage - Christ and the church

This biblical earthly marriage contract, or covenant, becomes a visual aid of the heavenly covenant. The ongoing relationship between a husband and wife is a picture of the relationship of Christ to his church.[28] The one flesh marriage act portrays the one flesh union of the believer and his Lord and prefigures the return of Christ when there will be the wedding supper of the Lamb.[29]

So the purpose of marriage is fivefold:-.

1. To bring mutual comfort and companionship
2. For the raising of children
3. To signify in its covenantal nature the ongoing relationship of Christ and the church
4. To signify in its one flesh union the believer's union with Christ
5. To prefigure Christ's return – the marriage supper of the Lamb

God has used symbols and picture language throughout Scripture that signify Christ and his work. Perhaps of all the examples in Scripture, marriage is the most enduring and vivid picture of Christ's ongoing ministry.

Divorce

Once the nature of the biblical marriage covenant has been understood, particularly its role in displaying to mankind the great redemptive theme of the relationship of Christ to his church, it becomes easier to understand on what basis the Bible allows divorce. It will be seen that throughout Scripture divorce is permitted (not commanded) when either the husband or the wife have signally failed in their covenantal roles, thus damaging the picture of Christ and the church.

---

[28] Ephesians 5:25-32
[29] Revelation 19:9

> **Key Points**
>
> - **Marriage is a picture of the relationship between Christ and the church**
>
> - **Marriage is a covenant relationship with gender based roles**
>
> - **Marriage is a heterosexual couple choosing to go through life together with a covenant of permanence (even if only implied), consummated with sexual intercourse.**

2 Marriage – a One Flesh Union

Paul tells us in Ephesians:-

After all, no one ever hated his own body, but he feeds and cares for it, just as Christ does the church for we are members of his body. "For this reason a man will leave his father and mother and be united to his wife, and the two will become one flesh." This is a profound mystery--but I am talking about Christ and the church. [30]

The nature of this one flesh union in marriage has to be considered in any treatment of divorce. The Roman Catholic Church and the Church of England have placed great weight on it in formulating their own positions.

The word 'mystery' used by Paul in Ephesians 5, when talking of the one flesh union of husband and wife, is the Greek word 'mysterion'. This was translated 'sacrament' from the (Latin) Vulgate translation of the Bible, a version widely used by the Roman Catholic Church for over a thousand years. The Roman Catholic community included marriage as a sacrament of the Church, to be conducted according to certain rituals.

In its classical Augustinian meaning a sacrament is a visible sign of an invisible grace - so it is believed God is present in the marriage in a real sense. In reality in many people's minds this means that something actually happens in heaven to endorse the earthly event – there is a mystical dimension. The Church of Rome takes the view there can be no divorce; God has 'endorsed' the marriage and nobody, not even the Pope himself, can authorize a divorce. The only way out of such a marriage is if it was viewed that the marriage was invalid, in which case it can be annulled, or more accurately declared to be null - deemed not to have taken place. The couple are then free to remarry. This teaching pervaded throughout Christendom until the Reformation.

---

[30] Ephesians 5:29-33

However a mystical view of marriage is present in the Church of England and is held widely (if subconsciously) even in the evangelical community. Andrew Cornes (a senior Anglican cleric) in his book 'Divorce and Remarriage' (endorsed by John Stott) states that:-

...a transformation takes place of which they [the couple being married] *are passive recipients, even though their choice and action set the transformation in motion; this transformation takes place not merely at the physical level, nor merely at the level of the emotions; it takes place at the deepest and most elemental level;* [31]

It is not clear precisely what Andrew Cornes means here when he describes the couple as being 'passively transformed', but this is very close to the Roman Church's position – only without the associated rituals. This thought process, that 'something happens in heaven' (or at least something mystical and intangible takes place on earth) when you marry, is reinforced by the modern secular view of 'love' and being 'in love' – that there is one person for you in this life and when you have found that person – and marry them – you have a marriage 'made in heaven'.

Jay Adams (a prominent evangelical Christian author in the USA) says:-

'*God's revealed goal for a husband and wife is to become one in all areas of their relationship – intellectually, emotionally, and physically.*' [32]

This sort of teaching places on the marriage union a weight that the biblical texts cannot bear. Why? Because the term

---

[31] Andrew Cornes 'Divorce and Remarriage' Eerdmans 1993 p61. Cornes, an Anglican vicar, was one time director of training at All Souls Langham Place. Cornes says his view of the one flesh union is 'not open to question'. This illustrates the strength of feeling commentators have about aspects of marriage teaching – and hence divorce – that cannot be specifically found in Scripture.
[32] 'Marriage Divorce and Remarriage in the Bible' Zondervan 1980 p17

'one flesh' (Hebrew:*basar*) in the Old Testament simply means one family – that husband and wife are now next of kin – they are a new family unit.[33]

Even Cornes concedes this as a definition for 'one flesh':-

*....it is possible that there is a further, more specific, meaning. Brown, Driver and Briggs lists **basar** in Genesis 2:24 under the meaning 'flesh', describing kindred, blood-relations. It is this which Wenham also argues for.* [34]

A constellation of Old Testament scholars argue for this straightforward meaning of the word. It is also the interpretation that best fits the scriptural context. Adam and Eve were the first one flesh family. God created Adam from the dust of the ground; he breathed into him and he became a living being. Then Eve was created from Adam; Adam was put into a deep sleep and she was formed from his side.

When Adam saw Eve he said:-

"This is now bone of my bones and flesh of my flesh; she shall be called 'woman,' for she was taken out of man." [35]

Eve was the very flesh and blood of Adam. The next words in the Bible narrative come from God:-

For this reason a man will leave his father and mother and be united to his wife, and they will become one flesh [36]

So all subsequent marriages are a re-creation of the one flesh union of the first couple. A new marriage creates a new family unit.

---

[33] See Heth 'Divorce and Remarriage' Paternoster Press 1984 p76ff. Also Instone-Brewer 'Divorce and Remarriage in the Bible' Eerdmans 2002 p22
[34] Op cit p61
[35] Genesis 2:23
[36] Genesis 2:24

Divorce and the Bible

The New Testament – the one flesh union explained

The New Testament does not change the meaning of the earthly one flesh union of marriage, using '*sarx*' the Greek word equivalent to *basar*. In the context of marriage this word also means kinship.[37]

But the New Testament does open up a fuller dimension of the significance of earthly marriage, by showing that it pictures a union of a believer to his God that **is** heavenly and mystical.

Of course like so many New Testament truths these things were prefigured in the Old, but the full glory of our adoption into the family of God is only in the New Testament. Just as Eve was literally one flesh with Adam – the church is figuratively one flesh with Christ. Indeed Paul compares and contrasts Adam to Christ. He tells us that as in Adam we all die – so in Christ we (the church) all shall live. [38]

In 1 Corinthians 15:45-49 he says:-

So it is written: "The first man Adam became a living being"; the last Adam, a life-giving spirit. The spiritual did not come first, but the natural, and after that the spiritual. The first man was of the dust of the earth, the second man from heaven. As was the earthly man, so are those who are of the earth; and as is the man from heaven, so also are those who are of heaven. And just as we have borne the likeness of the earthly man, so shall we bear the likeness of the man from heaven.

Eve came from Adam; she was bone of his bone, flesh of his flesh. Adam was a 'type' of Christ, Eve a 'type' of the church. Christ took on human flesh and the church in a mystical way becomes his body as Paul tells us earlier in his letter to the Corinthians: –

---

[37] See Vine's 'Expository Dictionary of New Testament Words' p448
[38] 1 Corinthians 15:22

Now you are the body of Christ, and each one of you is a part of it.[39]

Ephesians 5

Truly a believer is a family member. We can now see what Paul was saying in Ephesians 5:-

"For this reason a man will leave his father and mother and be united to his wife, and the two will become one flesh." This is a profound mystery--but I am talking about Christ and the church.[40]

The new family unit of man and wife is a picture of the relationship of Christ to his church. Our earthly marriages portray this heavenly reality. A 'mystery' in the writings of Paul, as many Bible commentators point out, means something that was previously hidden and is now revealed.

What had been hidden? Was it that the marriage relationship was a one flesh relationship? No - that had been clearly taught since the beginning. Was it that the husband and wife roles in marriage were a reflection of the covenantal relationship between God and his people? No – in the writings of the prophets God often compares himself to a husband of Israel.

The mystery revealed is the mystical one flesh union of the believer with his Lord and the fact that earthly marriage is a picture of that union. That is the new teaching.[41] The mystery in Ephesians 5 is not the marriage union – but how the marriage union can be a picture of the newly revealed truth of the union with Christ and his church. A point Hendriksen clearly makes in his commentary on Ephesians.[42] Paul does not say there are two mystical unions – one between a man and wife - and one between

---

[39] 1 Corinthians 12:27
[40] Ephesians 5:31-32
[41] Hebrews 3:5 refers to Moses as a servant in God's house – but Christians are God's children – 1 John 1:12.
[42] Hendriksen 'Ephesians' Banner of Truth 1972 p257

a believer and Christ. He simply says – *I am talking about Christ and the church*. One relationship is a picture of the other. This earthly marital relationship mirrors this heavenly theme.

The mystical element or 'transformation' in all of this lies not in the earthly marriage relationship, or in that the earthly marriage relationship causes something to happen in heaven, but that the earthly marriage relationship is a portrayal of the transformation that has happened in the heavenly dimension when a sinner comes to Christ.

Matthew 19 and Mark 10 – a heavenly marriage?

A careful look at the other relevant passages in the New Testament will show that they are similarly devoid of any reference to marriage in and of itself being a mystical or heavenly relationship. Jesus in Matthew 19 and Mark 10 states:-

'What God has put together, let man not separate.'

At first reading this seems to indicate that God has put the specific couple together – that he has married them - something has been effected in heaven by the contracting of this earthly marriage. The key however is in the understanding of 'man'. The New International Version is surely correct in using the phrase *'let man not separate'* - not *'let a man not separate'* – or even as the Church of England has it – *'let no man separate'*. What is being said here is that marriage is a God ordained institution with God ordained rules and 'man', as in 'mankind', is not to invent his own rules for divorce. Of course if we accept the Bible's teaching of God's all pervasive providence, there is a sense in which all marriages are put together by God, just as a sparrow does not fall to the ground without the will of the Father. [43] But to say that God is in heaven endorsing all the marriage unions on earth into some heavenly record is stretching the verse further than it will go.

---

[43] Matthew 10:29

In any case - which relationships are we to consider God has put together? Does God endorse in heaven relationships not sanctioned by the state or any recognised church – and if so which ones? Even if the definition of marriage given in the previous chapter is accepted [44] – who is to give the definitive answer as to which relationships qualify as a heavenly union?

1 Corinthians 6

Paul removes any doubt about the New Testament position in 1 Corinthians 6:-

15 Do you not know that your bodies are members of Christ himself? Shall I then take the members of Christ and unite them with a prostitute? Never! 16 Do you not know that he who unites himself with a prostitute is one with her in body? For it is said, "The two will become one flesh."
17 But he who unites himself with the Lord is one with him in spirit.
18 Flee from sexual immorality. All other sins a man commits are outside his body, but he who sins sexually sins against his own body. 19 Do you not know that your body is a temple of the Holy Spirit, who is in you, whom you have received from God? You are not your own; 20 you were bought at a price. Therefore honour God with your body. [45]

A believer has a mystical union with Christ – their bodies are the temple of the Holy Spirit. Paul does not say that an immoral believer is united in some spiritual way to the prostitute by his sexual immorality. In fact Paul's words show that is precisely what he is not saying – the immoral believer is one with her in **body** (v16) - but the Lord is one with him in **spirit** (v17).

---

[44] 'Marriage is a heterosexual couple choosing to go through life together with a covenant of permanence (even if only implied), consummated with sexual intercourse'
[45] 1 Corinthians 6:15-20

In fact Paul is even more specific in v16:

'Do you not know that he who unites himself with a prostitute is one with her in body....For it is said, "The two will become one flesh."

Therefore Paul gives the apostolic and definitive interpretation of the 'one flesh' of Genesis 2:24 and Matthew 19:6; it is a bodily, earthly (not heavenly), union. Paul's point is that if a believer takes what is holy and united to Christ – his redeemed body – and unites it with a prostitute in the sexual act – he is doing something particularly sinful.

Surely the sexual act in marriage is the most wondrous portrayal of both our present union with Christ and that glorious union yet to come when the church's relationship with Christ will be consummated at the marriage supper of the Lamb. For all these reasons the marriage act is 'sacred' – in the sense it is God-given, and serves as an exalted picture of our redemption story.

Little wonder that God has sought to protect this picture throughout earthly history, re-enforcing his commandments with the severe punishments of Leviticus and Deuteronomy. But it cannot be argued that the believer of 1 Corinthians 6 is actually becoming 'one flesh' (that is one family) with the prostitute, otherwise it would make him married to her – and by definition then the act would not be immoral. The immoral man is not creating a new family unit by the sex act with the prostitute.

Why not? Because God assumes throughout Scripture that the husband and wife will have a 'covenant' – an agreement – to reflect the covenant he had with Israel and he now has with his church; that the marriage relationship will be considered permanent with mutual expectations. The sex act alone does not establish such a covenant. As will be shown in Chapter 5, the sex act without a covenant is a sin that was subject to varying sanctions, the most serious being the death penalty.

If somebody puts on an army uniform it does not make him a soldier. A person may drive a car but it does not mean he has a licence. Marriage is a covenant consummated by sexual intercourse. One without the other is not marriage. None of this is to imply that because marriage itself is not mystical that marriage is mundane. The love of a man for a woman and a woman for a man, expressed within the marriage context becomes one of the most profound experiences of our mortal lives. Indeed it is the very richness and depth of this experience that has misled us. We confuse the many blessings of marriage with its purpose. It is like extolling a great meal, glorying in all the magnificent flavours and then saying this truly is the purpose of food.

Protected earthly symbols

Nor does it mean because marriage is a symbol of a heavenly reality, not the reality itself, that the symbol is unimportant. Throughout the Bible it is earthly pictures that are used to portray heavenly realities. [46] God uses many things to point us to Christ. In the Old Testament there was the whole sacrificial system, the tabernacle, [47] the brass serpent on the pole, [48] and the rock in the desert, [49] to name a few. In the New Testament there is baptism and communion.

Sometimes these symbols are fiercely protected. The ark of God was being brought back from the Philistines on a cart, the oxen stumbled, Uzzah reached out to steady it and was struck dead by God. Was the Lord of glory actually in that box on the ox cart? Was our Lord physically touched by Uzzah? But Uzzah paid with his life. [50]

Moses was forbidden the promised land for striking a rock in the desert. [51] Entrance to the promised land was to be the fulfilment of his life's work. Paul says the rock was Christ – but we do not believe it was literally Christ. Was the rock hurt? Did that lump of stone suffer an indignity? The

---

[46] This alone should have made us cautious about saying that marriage in itself is a mystical reality. It would be unusual if there was a heavenly reality – a mystical union of man and wife – to reflect another heavenly mystical union – that of Christ and the church.
[47] Exodus 25ff
[48] Numbers 21
[49] Numbers 20
[50] 2 Samuel 6
[51] Numbers 20 1 Corinthians 10:4

rock was a type of Christ – it pointed to our Saviour and as a consequence Moses was severely punished.

Similarly the evangelical believer does not believe that the bread and wine of our communion service actually becomes the body and blood of Christ. They are earthly symbols that point to our Saviour. But Paul warns us that:-

... whoever eats the bread or drinks the cup of the Lord in an unworthy manner will be guilty of sinning against the body and blood of the Lord [52]

In the same way marriage is an earthly picture of a heavenly reality – the heavenly reality of Christ's love for his people and an anticipation of consummation of that love that still awaits its fulfilment at the end of history. Earthly marriage and the expression of marital love help us to understand something of the love Christ has for us. A love that caused him to leave his heavenly Father to find, and cleave to, his church; securing her well-being in this age, and providing a home for her future.

It is the union of the believer with Christ that secures all the benefits of heaven. At the resurrection all the rites and rituals of the church, all our good works count for nothing - he will raise with him those who are his. [53] The union of the believer with Christ is the pinnacle of the redemption story. The focus of history is the wedding supper of the lamb when Christ will consummate his relationship with his church. The one flesh union of marriage is an earthly glimpse of that great event, yet not itself that event.

Adultery

That God is similarly fiercely protective of the symbolic picture that is marriage can be seen in the Bible's sanctions for adultery. The biblical definition of adultery is when a man has sexual intercourse with another man's wife (see Appendix 4). It will be seen that the penalty in the

---

[52] 1 Corinthians 11:27
[53] Romans 6:5

Pentateuch for this offence was death.

Why? The commentaries say it is because it 'breaks faith' with your marriage partner, it 'destroys marriages and homes', it 'breaks the one flesh union', it 'betrays the relationship' between husband and wife. And so it does, but the relationship it really betrays is that of Christ and the church. The church cannot be taken by another; Christ will not have his great work of redemption thwarted.

Just as Uzzah lost his life, Moses was forbidden the promised land, and we eat and drink damnation to ourselves if the Lord's supper is taken lightly, so the adulterer was condemned to death because he destroyed the picture of Christ's finished redemptive work.

Motivation and any subsequent contrition are not the issue. Uzzah thought he was doing right. If a husband was prepared to forgive his wife, and his wife was duly contrite and repentant - the law still said the death penalty was to be enforced. Why? Because the offence is not primarily against the marriages involved but against God - as Joseph so clearly states in Genesis 39:9. Contemporary Christian literature has taken a predominantly man-centred approach to divorce and has consequently missed this point.

The Sadducees' question

If this symbolic non-sacramental view of marriage is not the teaching of the Bible then there are considerable logistical problems in how God will (and does if we accept heaven as a reality now) work things out in heaven. Such considerations should not drive our interpretation of the verses, or our theology, but they ought to be considered, as they were by the Sadducees:-

That same day the Sadducees, who say there is no resurrection, came to him with a question. "Teacher," they said, "Moses told us that if a man dies without having children, his brother must marry the widow and have children for him. Now there were seven brothers among us. The first one married and died, and since he had no children, he left his wife to his brother. The same thing happened to the second and third brother, right on down to the seventh. Finally, the woman died. Now then, at the resurrection, whose wife will she be of the seven, since all of them were married to her? [54]

And Jesus' reply? :-

"You are in error because you do not know the Scriptures or the power of God. At the resurrection people will neither marry nor be given in marriage; they will be like the angels in heaven." [55]

In other words there is no married state in the life to come. Whatever the relationship between a husband and wife is in this life – it will not be so in the life to come. Of course behind the Sadducees' question was the fact they did not believe in a resurrection at all. But Jesus did not dismiss the premise of the question – that if there was such an after-life a woman who had had more than one husband would have a problem in heaven. Instead he tackled this real issue by clarifying that there is no marriage in heaven. The woman they describe will have no husband in heaven – except the Lord Jesus Christ himself. In other words there is no heavenly dimension to an earthly marriage except a symbolic one.

The Sadducees' question is not just a trick question to Jesus rooted in Jewish theology of the first century. It is a real question today. How do we explain a sacramental view of marriage to an unbelieving couple that have had the average five partners each (if modern statistics are to be believed), now converted, and are presenting themselves for marriage? What is the status of their previous relationships before God?

A mystical sacramental view of marriage cannot be consistently taught in this situation, unless it is believed that none of the previous relationships were marriage by any definition. At least the Roman Catholic Church is consistent in this aspect of its teaching about marriage and divorce.

---

[54] Matthew 22:23-28
[55] Matthew 22:29-30

Also if there are two mystical unions, one between a husband and wife, and another between a believer and his Lord, what of a mixed marriage, where one is a believer and one is not? It shall be seen that Paul describes these marriages as valid in God's eyes – indeed the unbelieving partner is 'sanctified' by the believer. But not saved by them. So under the sacramental teaching it would be possible to be mystically united with somebody who is eternally lost.

Conclusion

God given religious ceremonies and symbols are for our instruction, for our benefit not his, to teach us about heavenly realities, not to create heavenly realities themselves. A sacramental view of marriage has undoubtedly driven much divorce teaching for nearly two millennia. But nowhere does the Bible say that a man and woman when married become a new mystical entity. This teaching was introduced by the Church of Rome – they themselves accepting that it is not found in the Old Testament.

But the picture is not the reality. Adam was a type of Christ – he was not Christ or like Christ in any supernatural way, anymore than a husband is. And marriage is a picture, not a mystical reality - a supremely important picture that God does not want spoiled by marital breakdown. But such marital breakdowns are a fact of the fallen world which God recognised even in Moses' day.

However, many evangelical commentators have followed the sacramental path set by the Church of Rome, saying that Jesus promulgated a new doctrine about marriage (and consequently about divorce) that was never found in the Old Testament. In other words there is to be found a discontinuity between the Old and New Testament in this subject unique in all systematic biblical theology.

It will be seen in the next chapters that there is no such discontinuity – and once the sacramental view is left behind the New Testament teaching falls clearly into place.

Divorce and the Bible

Key Points

- **The 'one flesh' union of marriage means that the couple form a new family unit**

- **Marriage is not a sacrament and not a mystical union**

- **The sexual act without a 'covenant' is not marriage**

- **Marriage is a protected symbol of Christ and the church**

3 The Traditional Views

1.   No divorce at all

This is the Roman Catholic view. There are circumstances when they say the marriage was not 'valid' – and then declare the marriage to be 'annulled'.

2.   Divorce for sexual unfaithfulness but no remarriage

This until recently has been the Anglican view. More recently remarriage in church has been allowed to divorcees when the former spouse is still alive – but only in 'exceptional circumstances'. Among evangelicals it has been defended by Heth and Wenham. [56] Probably a minority view in evangelical circles.

3.   Divorce for sexual unfaithfulness and remarriage for the 'innocent' party

This is probably the view held by the majority in the evangelical churches.

4.   Divorce for sexual unfaithfulness and remarriage for either party

Although most commentators still assume an 'innocent' party some will allow remarriage of both parties.[57]

5.   Divorce when an unbelieving partner deserts

Based on the teaching of Paul in 1 Corinthians 7 many would accept this position, often in conjunction with 3 or

---

[56] 'Jesus and Divorce' Hodder & Stoughton 1984 Republished Paternoster Press 1997
[57] For example Instone-Brewer 'Divorce and remarriage in the Church' Paternoster Press 2003 p113-114. John Murray shows that the New Testament takes no position on the 'innocent' party - see 'Divorce' Presbyterian & Reformed 1961

Divorce and the Bible

4 above. So a believer could remarry if an unbelieving partner deserts.

6. Divorce for sundry reasons

A surprising number of commentators having worked out a biblical case for say numbers 3 and 5 above, then begin to add their own (often quite extensive) list of acceptable grounds for divorce. For example Keener in his final chapter includes certain criminal behaviours and physical or emotional abuse as grounds for the 'innocent' partner to divorce. [58] Even Heth (who in evangelical circles has some of the strictest views on divorce and remarriage) manages to find other grounds. [59]

Notwithstanding this the views numbered 3 through to 5 above are probably those most widely held today in the evangelical community. For the sake of brevity in the text these will be referred to as the 'traditional views'.

Key point

- **Probably the most widely held view about divorce in the evangelical community is:- Divorce for sexual unfaithfulness or desertion, and remarriage for the 'innocent' party**

---

[58] Keener '..and marries another' Hendrickson 1991. These grounds are not based on his biblical exposition but on pastoral experience. Why is it necessary to mount a detailed biblical argument for specific biblical grounds for divorce? Why not assume grounds based on pastoral experience and forget the biblical exegesis?
[59] 'Divorce and Remarriage' Inter Varsity Press 1990 p 59

4 The Thesis

The great themes of the Bible are creation, the Fall and redemption. Surely out of these three the great overarching theme is our redemption in Christ. It is indeed the greatest story ever told. It is the thrust and purpose of the Bible.

In this redemption story we see in the Old Testament God comparing himself to a husband, and Israel, his chosen people, to his wife. The New Testament specifically says that earthly marriage is to be a picture of Christ and the church. Right at the beginning of the Bible's account of our human story we are told:-

……….*a man will leave his father and mother and be united to his wife, and they will become one flesh.* [60]

And so Christ will leave his heavenly father to come for his church, and because of their union with him Christians can be assured of life with him in the world to come.

It has been seen in Chapter 1 that Scripture in teaching and practice shows that husbands and wives have different roles in marriage to reflect this great redemptive theme of mankind's history. Divorce is permitted when these roles – and rules – are broken. The Old and New Testament are consistent. Divorce is allowed when the redemptive picture of God and his bride Israel, Christ and his church, is spoiled.

The Old Testament position

- **A husband could (only) divorce his wife for her sexual impurity**

Deuteronomy 24 makes this clear. The picture is broken; the woman who was sexually impure was like Israel looking to an idol rather than the one true God. So the husband could divorce her.

---

[60] Genesis 2:24

Divorce and the Bible

- **A wife could divorce her husband if he is not faithful in his duty to provide**

In Exodus 21:10,11 a wife is entitled to 'food, clothing and marital rights'. In other words it might be said that she is entitled to material and emotional support. The passage teaches that if she does not receive them she is entitled to divorce her husband. Recent research has shown that this wording was alluded to in most Old Testament marriage contracts, and has been shown to be in Old Testament Israel the basis on which a wife could divorce her husband. [61]

Although these particular verses are ignored by most commentators, they are contained in the Pentateuch within a few verses of the Ten Commandments. Verse 11 says that if a wife was not provided for by her husband, she could go. In this case her husband had taken another wife and was failing in his duties.

The picture is clear. God provided Israel with all her needs, in turn all true Old Testament believers willingly embraced him. None were brought to faith in him, or held by him, against their will. Nor should a wife be bound to a husband against her will.

- **A husband could not divorce his wife for her failure to provide for him**

Exodus 21:10 shows that material and emotional support is the rightful expectation of the woman. There is no Old Testament verse anywhere which says a woman has to provide these things for her husband, or that a man can divorce his wife for her failure to provide them, or that there was any reason a husband could divorce his wife except for her sexual immorality.

---

[61] Instone-Brewer's published printed works, as well as those published on the internet, establish this position. Also see article by Judith Werner published in 'Women in Judaism: A Multidisciplinary Journal 2,1' 1999.

The Thesis

The New Testament position is – the same.

- **A husband is told that he can (only) divorce his wife for her sexual unfaithfulness**

Jesus, when asked about the position of men and divorce in Deuteronomy 24, repeats its teaching, clarifying that it was for sexual impurity alone that a man could divorce his wife. Jesus addressed the issues he was asked about – men and divorce in Deuteronomy 24. In that case the wife was divorced by her husband and had subsequently taken another husband – another 'Christ '– and could not come back to her first husband. She was 'apostate'. The picture is Christ and the church.

- **A wife can divorce her husband if he is not faithful in his duty to provide**

This is the clear teaching of Paul in 1 Corinthians 7 where the theme of Exodus 21 is reiterated. If the (unbelieving) husband has deserted her then Exodus 21 applies as he is not fulfilling his husbandly duties. She is to 'go free'. If she as an unbeliever deserts him then Exodus 21 still applies - she does not want to stay in the relationship – she is 'de facto' divorcing him. The exhortation given by Paul in 1 Corinthians 7:13 (..*and if a woman has a husband who is not a believer and he is willing to live with her, she must not divorce him*) presupposes that it was possible for a Christian wife to initiate a divorce against her husband for reasons other than – but including - his sexual unfaithfulness. Paul accepted the Exodus 21 position. No believer is held to Christ against their will.

- **A husband cannot divorce his wife for her failure to provide for him**

- or any other reason apart from sexual impurity. In 1 Corinthians 7 if a Christian husband is deserted by his wife she has effectively taken the initiative and divorced him as she is allowed to do in Exodus 21. There is no New Testament verse which says the Christian (or non-Christian) husband is allowed to initiate a divorce of his wife for her failure to provide for him. The church does not provide for Christ and Christ will not forsake his church.

In summary:-

- There is no change between Old and New Testament teaching.

- There is no contradiction between Jesus and Paul and Paul's teaching is not a new departure – it is not the 'Pauline exception'.

- No woman is to be held in a marriage against her will, any more than a believer is held by Christ against their will.

- If a husband is faithful to his task and cares for his wife as Christ cares for the church she has no basis for divorce.

- No man may 'put away' his wife for any cause whatsoever – except marital unfaithfulness. Why? Because Christ will hold on to the church through all her troubles and only if she wilfully walks away from him will he 'deny' her.

- The Bible is consistent, clear, and majestic in its teaching about divorce as it is in its teaching about marriage.

- God hates divorce. Why? Because it breaks the picture of Christ and the church.

Why has this not been the teaching of the church?

- The covenantal nature of marriage has been largely lost

The majority of houses in the UK are built of bricks and mortar. The bricks give the house shape and function, the mortar helps keep it all together. The bricks are like the covenant of the marriage, the mortar is like the romantic, emotional, and sexual relationship of the couple. A house of nothing but mortar can have no distinct shape and would be soon washed away in a storm. Today's wedding vows are based on the romantic, sexual, and mutual help aspect of the relationship, not - 'what is my role?' – 'what is expected of me in this relationship?'. This perspective has come right into the church. As a consequence divorce teaching is based primarily on the failure of these emotional aspects of the relationship – not about a failure in the covenantal role. The latter is the Bible's emphasis.

- the wrong assumptions have been made

When expounding the gospel statements commentators have looked to harmonise what they perceived as the unfair position of wives, (where it was thought they could not divorce their husbands) compared with that of husbands. John Murray, unlike many, does make it clear in his work that he is making an assumption not found in the text:-

'..surely it is necessary to believe...the same rights and liberties are granted to the woman as are granted to the man' [62]

It is hoped to show that with this assumption an exegesis is forced onto the text which actually does harm to women and to God's intentions.

- the church has been ambivalent about human sexuality

As a consequence any position on marriage or divorce that seemed to be more 'strict' has often been considered to be more in line with God's will. This can be seen right from the earliest days when some in the Corinthian church asked the apostle Paul about abstaining from sex - many

---

[62] 'Divorce' Presbyterian & Reformed 1961 See pp96-98. This comment specifically on Mark 10:12 p97

commentators take it that they were referring to sex within marriage. Paul had to correct this view. In the 3rd century one of the church fathers – Origen of Alexandria - famously castrated himself seeing Matthew 19:12 in a literal sense.

In the 13th century Thomas Aquinas, an influential Roman Catholic theologian, said:-

"Even married sex, adorned with all the honourableness of marriage, carries with it a certain shame....Without a doubt the state of virginity is preferable." [63]

The discovery in the 20th century of the Dead Sea scrolls unearthed the writings of the Essenes, a Jewish group of the first century. When they extolled the virtues of one wife it was thought they were saying it is best not to re-marry after a divorce or the death of a spouse. A view that Cornes is close to today. [64] It is now known that the Essenes were speaking against having more than one wife at a time. [65]

Does it matter?

The implications of bringing secular ideas of fairness and equality into divorce are considerable. (Fortunately for fallen man the Bible's emphasis is more on grace and mercy than fairness and equality.) If the grounds for divorce are the same for husbands and wives an important biblical picture that God has sought to preserve throughout his dealings with us is lost. A wife, under this traditional teaching, is restricted, in that she can only divorce her husband for his sexual unfaithfulness – specifically for most commentators that means sexual intercourse with another woman - and for no other reason whatsoever. In this situation a wife is left in a vulnerable position. Most commentators when they deal with the pastoral problems of divorce acknowledge this difficulty.

---

[63] Summa Theologica 2.2 151 -152
[64] Cornes 'Divorce and Remarriage' Eerdmans 1993 p275ff
[65] See Collins 'Divorce in the New Testament' Liturgical Press 1992 p194

The Bible really is clear

Divorce is the reverse image of marriage, so the fundamental basis for divorce teaching is how it impacts the picture that marriage is meant to be, that is of Christ and the church. Even without that framework of interpretation it will be seen that this thesis contains a straightforward unforced exegesis of the relevant texts.

> **Key points**
>
> - **Exodus 21 outlines the rules for a woman initiating a divorce against her husband**
>
> - **Deuteronomy 24 outlines the rules for a man initiating a divorce against his wife**
>
> - **Jesus emphasises principles and answers the specific question he was asked**
>
> - **1 Corinthians 7 permits either a husband or wife to treat their partner's desertion as a divorce**

5 The Old Testament and Divorce

Genesis 21:9-12

But Sarah saw that the son whom Hagar the Egyptian had borne to Abraham was mocking, and she said to Abraham, "Get rid of that slave woman and her son, for that slave woman's son will never share in the inheritance with my son Isaac." The matter distressed Abraham greatly because it concerned his son. But God said to him, "Do not be so distressed about the boy and your maidservant. Listen to whatever Sarah tells you, because it is through Isaac that your offspring will be reckoned.

Abraham took Hagar as a second wife to have the child that God had promised to Sarah and himself. Is this then the first divorce? And if it is, what does this event teach us today? Here we learn about the mind of God, the outworking of sin, and God's sovereign purposes. But this verse does not teach us any principles about divorce, any more than God's instruction to Abraham to sacrifice his son Isaac can teach us about child care. God instructed Abraham to divorce Hagar for his own purposes at this particular point in redemptive history; this does not establish a teaching about grounds for divorce.

Exodus 21:7-11

"If a man sells his daughter as a servant, she is not to go free as menservants do. If she does not please the master who has selected her for himself, he must let her be redeemed. He has no right to sell her to foreigners, because he has broken faith with her. If he selects her for his son, he must grant her the rights of a daughter. If he marries another woman, he must not deprive the first one of her food, clothing and marital rights. If he does not provide her with these three things, she is to go free, without any payment of money."

The situation in these verses is that a man sells his daughter into slavery in the expectation that either the master, or the master's son, will marry her. If they do not she is not to be sold to foreigners. If the master marries her, but then marries another woman, the first (slave) wife is not to be denied food, clothes or marital rights.

Another passage that cannot really be applied to us?

Western society generally does not have slaves or 'sell' people – or have second wives. These facts mean most commentators leave this verse alone; many books from within the Christian community have been written about divorce in the Old Testament but few consider Exodus 21. But this passage cannot be dismissed lightly. The principles found in this chapter have been widely applied in our society – principles about intentional and unintentional injury, kidnap, the punishment to fit the crime, what today is called public liability - and so on. The original status of the first wife as a slave had no bearing on her position in the marriage.[66] Also the Pentateuch legislates for a second wife in the Old Testament economy so the plural marriage in Exodus 21 was a legal institution. [67] And significantly, there is a repetition of the principle of a husband's responsibility to his wife as outlined in Exodus 21, in Ephesians 5 where a husband is told, in a comparison to Christ and his care for the church, that he should 'feed and care for' his wife:-

Husbands, love your wives, just as Christ loved the church and gave himself up for her to make her holy, cleansing her by the washing with water through the word, and to present her to himself as a radiant church, without stain or wrinkle or any other blemish, but holy and blameless. In this same way, husbands ought to love their wives as their own bodies. He who loves his wife loves himself. After all,

---

[66] See Satlow 'Jewish Marriage in Antiquity' p195
[67] For example Deuteronomy 21:15-17. Stephen Clark states that a second wife is not illegal but unlawful. See 'Putting Asunder Divorce and Remarriage in Biblical and pastoral perspective' Bryntirion Press 1999 p26

no one ever hated his own body, but he feeds and cares for it, just as Christ does the church [68]

Also David Instone-Brewer has convincingly shown in his book 'Divorce and Remarriage in the Bible', and elsewhere, that these Exodus verses are of considerable importance. Stephen Clark says of Dr Instone-Brewer's work on these verses:-

Brewer has drawn attention to the significance of Exodus 21:10-11 (Brewer Tyndale Bulletin 47.1 [1996], pp7-12). I am not aware of treatments of divorce, from a Christian perspective, which consider the significance of these verses. In this respect, Brewer has broken new ground and has placed us greatly in his debt. He draws attention to the fact that these verses are referred to in several Jewish marriage contracts, and alluded to in most of them. Moreover he demonstrates that the terms of the marriage contract found in these verses are referred to by Biblical authors as well as by the early rabbis. Most significantly, the final words of verse 11, 'she is to go free', form the basis of Jewish divorce certificates. The passage has clearly figured in Jewish treatments of divorce, though not largely in Christian teaching. However, Christian commentators have long been aware that these verses are dealing with divorce. Thus Matthew Poole, the Puritan commentator, clearly regards these verses as giving the woman a right of divorce where she has not been provided with food, clothing or conjugal duties. (Poole, vol1, pp162-3).See also comments by Durham. [69]

So what is the principle about divorce here? The husband is to provide for the first slave wife, not to neglect her. But the second wife's rights are not mentioned. Is it not the

---

[68] Ephesians 5:25-29
[69] 'Putting Asunder Divorce and Remarriage in Biblical and pastoral perspective' Bryntyrion Press1999 p230. Subsequently in 'Foundations' published by Affinity, Spring 2004 p44 he casts doubt on the application of the Exodus 21 passage saying that not sufficient account is taken in Instone-Brewer's work of Christ's 'eschatological fulfilment'. Surely Christ fulfilled shadows and types, he did not reverse principles.

The Old Testament and Divorce

wisdom of God that he knows a man's heart? The husband will be inclined to nurture his new wife and neglect the first, so God addresses his comments to the husband about his first wife. God would not surely mean by this that he can neglect his second new wife. It is a legitimate expectation for each wife to be provided for by their husband with food, clothing and marital rights. And if either does not get them – they are to 'go free', they can divorce their husband.

Assumptions are assumptions

This is an early example of something that will be encountered several times and will be dealt with more fully in Chapter 6. It is possible to make assumptions about the statement in Exodus 21:10 based on contextual circumstances and what is known of the character of God as revealed elsewhere in Scripture. I hope you will agree that the assumption about the rights of the second wife is a reasonable one to make. The difficulty arises when other assumptions are made that are less well founded. A clear example of this is when Dr Instone-Brewer in his book 'Divorce & Remarriage in the Church' says:-

..if a wife had these rights, then a husband was also entitled to the same right to divorce a wife who neglected him [70]

Dr Instone-Brewer is hugely knowledgeable in this area and his assumption seems a simple and reasonable one. The impression received on reading his book is that this was the accepted practice in Judaism at this time.

No matter how reasonable, it was not the Jewish practice, nor is it the biblical position. There is no instance in the Bible by instruction or example of a wife having to provide for her husband – and of course it breaks the picture of Christ and the church. [71] Only in his much larger

---

[70] Paternoster Press 2003 Page 25
[71] The wife of Proverbs 31 is an example of a godly woman serving her family. But I do not believe that it can be deduced that she had ultimate responsibility of providing for her herself and family. If this was the case it is difficult to see in the culture of the time that her husband would be 'respected at the gate' – v23

and somewhat less accessible work, 'Divorce & Remarriage in the Bible', are we told:-

Only a small number of Jewish marriage certificates have survived from the first centuries [after Christ] ……..*All of them contain a phrase referring to the obligations to clothe and feed. Like Greco-Roman contracts, these obligations are incumbent only on the man…….*[72]

Mutual obligations only came much later in Judaism, in fact it seems not until well into the Christian era. It is not surprising that when such 'reasonable' but non-biblical assumptions are made that God's intentions are obscured.

'To go free'

The first wife in the context of Exodus 21 can divorce her husband and she is to 'go free'. She is 'freed' by him to remarry. This is what was understood by this expression at the time. [73] A Jewish woman then (and today) could initiate a divorce from her husband, especially for lack of marital rights. But unless her husband releases her by signing the relevant divorce certificate she is unable to remarry, she is '*agunah*' – literally 'chained' or 'bound'. There are many Jewish women today who are divorced - but *agunah* - they are not free, their husbands have not released them, having not signed the relevant certificate.[74] Exodus 21 is saying the wife is to be given the proper divorce certificate that meant she was free to remarry. The issue of remarriage after divorce will be addressed in Chapter 8.

'Without any payment of money'

The Jewish system was that a prospective husband had

---

[72] Eerdmans 2002 page 215. Dr Instone-Brewer then speculates for some pages why this anomaly might be, not seemingly considering it is part of the divine plan
[73] Instone-Brewer 'Divorce and Remarriage in the Bible' Eerdmans 2002 Chapter 2 & p117ff
[74] See Appendix 5: Agunah

to pay the father of the bride a 'bride price'. Several commentators see an abusive patriarchal society at work here, treating the woman as a possession to be 'sold'. [75] Is it not rather a husband 'purchasing' his bride as Christ did the church? Some cultures even today have this system (for example Madagascar). However there is also often a dowry given by the bride's family that had to be returned if there was a divorce, unless the husband was divorcing her for sexual unfaithfulness. But in the case of a slave wife she would not have brought a dowry, so the husband did not have to pay any money back. [76] The slave wife was allowed to go free, she had the same rights as the 'free' wife, but she had brought no money to the relationship so she was not entitled to make a claim on the husband's estate if she was initiating the divorce.

What is a fair provision?

Who is to decide what constituted a fair provision of food, clothes and marital rights? The Bible does not stipulate, but this did not deter the rabbis. Over the years they tried to specify precisely what a fair provision was, often rather amusingly, and therefore what constituted grounds for a divorce. [77] Much would surely depend on cultural factors and the couple's particular circumstances? How could a 'list' or standard be given? It is a very individual thing. Is it really impossible to think that the wife could decide? Look at the verse again. Where does it say that the rabbi, the husband – or any one else is to have the decision? No – 'if he does not.... she is to go free'. Surely only she could know.

It does seem in the Old Testament that divorce was essentially a private matter, as it is in Judaism today. If Exodus 21 is compared with Deuteronomy 24 there is no

---

[75] For example 'Marriage & Divorce' Alex Deasley Beacon Hill Press 2000 p44
[76] p23 Instone-Brewer 'Divorce and Remarriage in the Bible' Eerdmans 2002
[77] Instone-Brewer 'Divorce and Remarriage in the Church' Paternoster Press 2003 p90

mention of an outside tribunal. It was the husband who wrote the certificate of divorce – not any court.

Deuteronomy 21:10-14

"When you go to war against your enemies and the LORD your God delivers them into your hands and you take captives, if you notice among the captives a beautiful woman and are attracted to her, you may take her as your wife. Bring her into your home and have her shave her head, trim her nails and put aside the clothes she was wearing when captured. After she has lived in your house and mourned her father and mother for a full month, then you may go to her and be her husband and she shall be your wife. If you are not pleased with her, let her go wherever she wishes. You must not sell her or treat her as a slave, since you have dishonoured her."

This looks a bleak situation from our modern viewpoint – however this would have been the height of compassion in comparison to what happened in the nations surrounding Israel at this time. But again it is the principle not the specific situation we are considering.

The man is allowed to take her as a wife – and let her go if he is not pleased with her. The verse does not say what displeasure constituted sufficient grounds for divorce – but we are told within a few chapters (Deuteronomy 24) that for 'displeasure' to be grounds for divorce it had to be based on her sexual impurity. It is only reasonable to assume that the same applies here. If this was not the case the Jewish male would surely have made this verse a 'cause celebre' for divorcing their wives for any reason. They did not – instead they tried to use the slightly unusual wording in Deuteronomy 24 to achieve that end.

Deuteronomy 22:13-19

If a man takes a wife and, after lying with her, dislikes her and slanders her and gives her a bad name, saying, "I married this woman, but when I approached her, I did not find proof of her virginity," then the girl's father and *mother shall bring proof that she was a virgin to the town elders at the gate. The girl's father will say to the elders, "I gave my daughter in marriage to this man, but he dislikes her. Now he has slandered her and said, `I did not find your daughter to be a virgin.' But here is the proof of my daughter's virginity." Then her parents shall display the cloth before the elders of the town, and the elders shall take the man and punish him. They shall fine him a hundred shekels of silver and give them to the girl's father, because this man has given an Israelite virgin a bad name. She shall continue to be his wife; he must not divorce her as long as he lives.*

The husband has falsely accused his wife of not being a virgin when he married her and as a consequence he has to pay the fine – and the natural reading is that he could not then divorce her for **any** reason – not even sexual impurity. Perhaps having falsely accused her once of sexually impurity he could not be relied on to get it right on any subsequent occasion.

Deuteronomy 22:28-29

If a man happens to meet a virgin who is not pledged to be married and rapes her and they are discovered, he shall pay the girl's father fifty shekels of silver. He must marry the girl, for he has violated her. He can never divorce her as long as he lives.

Again, having abused the woman once, the man is not allowed ever to divorce her.

Deuteronomy 24:1-4

If a man marries a woman who becomes displeasing to him because he finds something indecent about her, and he writes her a certificate of divorce, gives it to her and sends her from his house, and if after she leaves his house she becomes the wife of another man, and her second husband dislikes her and writes her a certificate of divorce, gives it to her and sends her from his house, or if he dies, then her

Divorce and the Bible

first husband, who divorced her, is not allowed to marry her again after she has been defiled. That would be detestable in the eyes of the LORD. Do not bring sin upon the land the LORD your God is giving you as an inheritance.

There has been much focus on this passage in many books about divorce. The first point is that this passage is not actually primarily about divorce per se. It is saying that a woman, having been divorced by her husband, if she subsequently marries another, cannot then go back to her first husband whatever the circumstance of the split from her second husband. It is a remarkable fact that few commentators even mention this – and those that do struggle to come up with a reason why. Six different interpretations are offered by Heth.[78] The second point about this passage, also not often mentioned, is that the woman, who is the 'guilty' party, is allowed to remarry. This surely should sound a warning note for those that believe that only the 'innocent' party is allowed to remarry. [79]

The third point – and this is where the Pharisees were coming from who questioned the Lord – is that a reason for the man divorcing his wife is given – albeit in passing, and (at least from the perspective of the Pharisees) somewhat ambiguously. The problem lies in the phrase in v1 - translated '*something indecent*' in NIV. This has been extensively covered effectively by many writers on this subject, but briefly, there were two opinions in our Lord's day. One group (the Hillelites) believed that this meant that a man could divorce his wife for virtually any cause. The other group (the Shammaites) thought it was divorce only for sexual impurity. Not surprisingly it became known as the '*any cause*' debate.

That divide is reflected today in Christian commentaries. Some agree with Hillel that the passage is about some arbitrary thing that displeased a husband - that Moses was allowing husbands to divorce their wives

---

[78] 'Divorce and Remarriage' IVP 1990 p83ff
[79] Although it was rabbinic teaching that a woman could not marry the man she had committed adultery with. 'Divorce & Remarriage in the Bible' Instone-Brewer Page 210

for trivial reasons.[80] An argument often used by those that hold this view is that the phrase cannot refer to sexual impurity, because the penalty for adultery was death, so any discussion of divorce was pointless; Deuteronomy is not talking of sexual sins at all – but some arbitrary thing that displeased the husband.

But this argument confuses sexual impurity with adultery. Sexual impurity by a wife might embrace many things including a lesbian relationship, or bestiality, or inappropriate nakedness. Some commentators lend weight specifically to the latter in this Deuteronomy passage. In contrast adultery (*na'aph*) was a very specific form of sexual impurity – that of a wife having heterosexual intercourse with someone other than her husband - for which we shall see the death penalty was not always enforced.

Others agree with Shammaite that the passage is about sexual impurity; many commentators have made detailed arguments to support this view.[81] It is not intended to rehearse all the points made in favour of this interpretation here, but the word ' *'erwat* ' – is used in Leviticus 18 to refer to the nakedness involved in the forbidden sexual relationships listed there, and similarly in Ezekiel 16 where the word is used to refer to the shame of nakedness.

Also this is an instance where it is helpful to consider the spiritual truth signified. If marriage is a picture of our relationship with God, on what grounds would he sever that relationship? It seems clear from many references in the Old Testament that God considered Israel's idolatry to be adultery – and threatened to 'divorce' them for it. This will be looked at below. So God would divorce his 'wife' for 'sexual impurity' – specifically that of 'adultery'.

So you might well expect, for the picture to hold, that he only allows men to divorce their wives for sexual impurity. It would run counter to this to assume that Moses allowed divorce for some arbitrary reason – and there

---

[80] See Jay Adams 'Marriage, Divorce and Remarriage in the Bible' Zondervan 1980. Also Stephen Clark who suggests that it might refer to a husband no longer finding his wife physically attractive. 'Putting Asunder...' Bryntirion Press 1999 p29.
[81] For example Instone-Brewer, Keener, Heth, Wenham, Cornes, and Kostenberger.

seems no overriding exegetical reason to support such a view. [82] Surely NIV has chosen a good phrase - *'something indecent'*. (For a fuller consideration of Deuteronomy 24 see Appendix 1, where thirteen reasons are given to show that the view that Moses allowed divorce for trivial reasons is a highly unlikely interpretation of the passage.)

So a wife could (not must) be divorced by her husband for her sexual impurity. This is an important Old Testament principle that Jesus reaffirms. She was free to remarry, and it will be seen that Jesus did not withdraw that right.

Why was there no going back for this wife?

Why was the wife not allowed to return to her first husband – why was it 'detestable in the eyes of the Lord'? Surely it is a warning against apostasy.

In **Jeremiah 3:1** we read:-

If a man divorces his wife and she leaves him and marries another man, should he return to her again? Would not the land be completely defiled? But you have lived as a prostitute with many lovers-- would you now return to me?" declares the LORD.

And **Jeremiah 3:8:-**

I gave faithless Israel her certificate of divorce and sent her away because of all her adulteries. Yet I saw that her unfaithful sister Judah had no fear; she also went out and committed adultery.

So God considers the application of his own rules on earthly marriage and divorce, in the relationship he had with Israel, a heavenly forgiving husband with a wayward wife. Jeremiah is warning Israel about her idolatry and apostasy, that she must not presume God will take her back to him after he

---

[82] Surely Kostenberger is correct in saying '*..since marriage was held in high esteem in ancient Israel, the offence was surely not merely trivial...*' 'God Marriage and Family' Crossway 2004 p 228

has divorced her. Judah we are told should have feared this prospect.

Is it too much for us to see Christ and the church in this Deuteronomy 24 passage? [83] If a woman wilfully walks away from her husband with her sinful behaviour, and takes another husband – another 'saviour' – she cannot surely then come back? Is this not what the New Testament teaches in its many warnings about apostasy?

Many Christians love the great Reformation doctrines and see that they are safe in Jesus' hands - but should there not be a fear of apostasy? And note that in Deuteronomy 24 it is not the sexual sin, it is not sexual intercourse with another man that denies her a return to her husband. Jesus made it clear that a sinning wife could be forgiven; a backsliding Christian will be welcomed back into the fold.

No, the important point is that the woman in Deuteronomy 24 was divorced by her first husband because of her sexual impurity and then took another husband. She was entitled to do this, but in the spiritual picture she repudiated her first husband, her 'Christ', by marrying another. So in the picture language she was denying the one and only Christ. This is not to say any woman that divorces her husband, or who is divorced by her husband and marries another is 'lost'. It is simply that God used this situation to teach a spiritual truth; apostates will not return to Christ.

Reading this passage with this perspective it is possible to recall these words from Hebrews 6:4-6:-

It is impossible for those who have once been enlightened, who have tasted the heavenly gift, who have shared in the Holy Spirit, who have tasted the goodness of the word of God and the powers of the coming age, if they fall away, to be brought back to repentance, because to their loss they are crucifying the Son of God all over again and subjecting him to public disgrace.

---

[83] No commentator I have read to date makes this connection, not even Heth with his six interpretations

Christians ought not to be like Judah – they should have a godly fear of apostasy and order their lives accordingly.

Besides Jeremiah, other prophets compare God's covenant with Old Testament Israel to a marriage.

Hosea

The picture in Hosea again is God, the long suffering husband, Israel the unfaithful wife. Hosea is asked to live out this relationship in his own life – to experience first hand what it was like for God to have a faithless 'wife'. Here is not the place to expound Hosea to consider whether this was a literal relationship, whether Hosea really divorced his wife and then took her back contrary to Deuteronomy 24. This is all open to conjecture. But the picture is nonetheless clear.

Isaiah

In Isaiah Jerusalem/Israel is often personified as a woman – as a wife, and God as her husband.

Malachi

In Malachi 2:10-12 we read:-

Have we not all one Father? Did not one God create us? Why do we profane the covenant of our fathers by breaking faith with one another? Judah has broken faith. A detestable thing has been committed in Israel and in Jerusalem: Judah has desecrated the sanctuary the LORD loves, by marrying the daughter of a foreign god. As for the man who does this, whoever he may be, may the LORD cut him off from the tents of Jacob--even though he brings offerings to the LORD Almighty.

Ezra

As the exiled Jews came back to re-establish temple worship in Jerusalem, Ezra insisted that the men send any foreign wives away. [84] They were effectively told to divorce their wives. Ezra is the only place in the Bible that we read that men were commanded to separate from their wives – and that not for sexual immorality. Many Jewish men at the time had married 'foreign' women. As with Hagar this was a specific time in Israel's history. Ezra issued this instruction to that group of people; it was not a general rule.

Lessons to be learned

- **For him – a wife's immorality is the only grounds for divorce**

So the prophets are consistent. Even in their picture language, using the analogy of marriage, divorce from God was on the grounds of the 'immorality' of his 'wife'.

In Malachi we read that God hates divorce. There is no inconsistency here. Divorce was not commanded for unfaithfulness anywhere in the Old Testament – what was commanded was the issue of a divorce certificate if a man was divorcing his wife, so that his wife could go free. It was never God's intention that there should be divorce, any more than it was God's intention that Adam should disobey him in the Garden of Eden.

The main principle is that the marriage relationship is a picture of God and Israel, and Israel's idolatry and waywardness is compared to a wife who is sexually unfaithful to her husband. So a wife is to be sexually faithful to her husband for the picture of God and Israel to hold together. If she is not, the husband can divorce her as God threatened to do with Israel, and depending on your eschatology, actually did.

- **For her – she can go free**

In Western society the tradition is to bind each other in marriage by statute law, so the principle that divorce is a

---

[84] Ezra 10:11

private matter, as the Pentateuch suggests, seems strange. But if a wife does not want the marriage to continue, if she is not willing to stay with her husband – then surely neither he nor anyone else should try to compel her to do so?

In his great book 'The Bondage of the Will', Luther shows us that man's problem is not just that he does not want God, but that left to himself he would never choose the Lord Jesus Christ. But God does not force the sinner to come to him, instead he changes his will. In a mysterious operation of the Holy Spirit, a sinner's heart and mind is changed, so that they are drawn irresistibly to Christ. The details cannot be pressed, but surely in some way the husband is to imitate his Saviour in that he does not force his wife, but instead (in this earthly type) by his winsome behaviour woos her to win her, and so makes marriage to him the thing she most wants to have – and to keep. So the picture of Christ and the church is preserved.

What conclusions can be drawn?

- Marriage, and so divorce, is a picture of a great spiritual truth
- A husband could divorce his wife only for sexual impurity
- A wife can divorce her husband for his failure to provide
- In both cases the divorce itself was not sinful; there was freedom to remarry with no restriction on the 'guilty' party
- God hates divorce

It should not surprise us to find, knowing that our God does not change, and that the Lord Jesus Christ is the Word of God incarnate, that these teachings are all repeated and reinforced in the New Testament.

There is not the discontinuity between the Testaments in their teaching about divorce that the traditional views demand.

Key Points

- **Divorce was allowed by God after the Fall of man and is not in itself sinful**

- **The Old Testament rules governing divorce are gender specific**

- **Divorce for the man is allowed if his wife is sexually unfaithful**

- **Divorce for the woman is allowed if in her own opinion her husband is not faithful to his task**

6 Jesus and Divorce

What Jesus actually said:-

Two statements:

Matthew 5:31

It has been said, `Anyone who divorces his wife must give her a certificate of divorce.' But I tell you that anyone who divorces his wife, except for marital unfaithfulness, causes her to become an adulteress, and anyone who marries the divorced woman commits adultery.

Luke 16:18

"Anyone who divorces his wife and marries another woman commits adultery, and the man who marries a divorced woman commits adultery."

And an answer to a question:

Matthew 19:3 - 11

Some Pharisees came to him to test him. They asked, "Is it lawful for a man to divorce his wife for any and every reason?"
    "Haven't you read," he replied, "that at the beginning the Creator `made them male and female,' and said, `For this reason a man will leave his father and mother and be united to his wife, and the two will become one flesh'? So they are no longer two, but one. Therefore what God has joined together, let man not separate."
    "Why then," they asked, "did Moses command that a man give his wife a certificate of divorce and send her away?"
    Jesus replied, "Moses permitted you to divorce your wives because your hearts were hard. But it was not this way from the beginning. I tell you that anyone who divorces his

wife, except for marital unfaithfulness, and marries another woman commits adultery."

Mark 10:2-12

Some Pharisees came and tested him by asking, "Is it lawful for a man to divorce his wife?" "What did Moses command you?" he replied. They said, "Moses permitted a man to write a certificate of divorce and send her away."

"It was because your hearts were hard that Moses wrote you this law," Jesus replied. "But at the beginning of creation God `made them male and female.' `For this reason a man will leave his father and mother and be united to his wife, and the two will become one flesh.' So they are no longer two, but one. Therefore what God has joined together, let man not separate."

When they were in the house again, the disciples asked Jesus about this. He answered, "Anyone who divorces his wife and marries another woman commits adultery against her. And if she divorces her husband and marries another man, she commits adultery."

The Old Testament Background – two facts to grasp

Whatever the views of the reader about the position outlined in the previous chapter and the applications, if any, that it is felt can be made in the Christian era, the overwhelming evidence in Judaism of first century Palestine is that a wife could divorce her husband, and grounds for divorce were gender specific.

- **a wife could divorce her husband**

The right of a wife to initiate a divorce was the unanimous position of the rabbis – and is the situation in much of the Jewish community today. Satlow (writing from a Jewish perspective) when considering the nature of God's covenant with Israel says that:-

'Because the relationship is mutual either partner should have the right to divorce. Biblical [Old Testament] legislation appears to confirm... these implications.' [85]

What has seemingly confused many commentators is that while a wife could divorce her husband, he had to sign a certificate of divorce otherwise she was left in a sort of no-man's land unable to remarry. (See Appendix 5: Agunah). Although Jewish men have abused this system, the certificate itself was a perfectly sensible requirement in that it showed the ex-husband had no further claim on her – or she on him. The modern UK equivalent would be a decree absolute issued by the court. With the increasing levels of cohabitation in the West it is to be wondered whether couples should not be adopting this Old Testament practice and signing some sort of release letter for each other.

- **grounds for divorce were gender specific**

In the Old Testament, and in the Lord's day, grounds for divorce really were gender specific. As was seen in the last chapter, all the biblical and extra-biblical evidence unequivocally shows this. Every Old Testament verse speaking of divorce deals with husbands and wives separately – and differently. There were two grounds for divorce; for the husband - if his wife was sexually impure; for the wife – for unreasonable behaviour by her husband. It can be seen that the husband's grounds for divorce were much more narrow than that for the wife. However with the teaching of Hillel many had come to believe that the correct interpretation of Deuteronomy was that a husband could divorce his wife for 'any cause'.[86]

---

[85] Satlow 'Jewish Marriage in Antiquity' p44 Princeton University Press 2001

[86] The Mishnah though only compiled around AD 200 says: *The school of Shammai say: A man may not divorce his wife unless he has unchastity in her, for it is written ,"Because he has found in her indecency in anything" (Deut.24:1). And the school of Hillel say:[He may divorce her] even if she spoiled a dish for him, for it is written, "Because he has found in her indecency in anything"* (m.Gittin 9:10)

Jesus and Divorce

This was the great divorce debate in first century Palestine and full weight must be given to it when considering the New Testament teaching – where it will be seen that Jesus also addresses husbands and wives separately – and differently. But so strong is the mindset of commentators that the Bible must teach gender 'sameness' - this is either not considered or even commented on in their own work.[87]

The sounds of silence

The gospels record Jesus making only three statements about divorce. One is recorded in Matthew 5:31-32, one in Luke 16:18, and the other is Jesus' answer to a question, recorded in Matthew 19:3-11 and Mark 10:2-12. In Mark and Luke he seems to forbid divorce for any reason. In both statements in Matthew he allows an exception, saying if the wife is sexually impure divorce was allowed. The brevity of these pronouncements has led to many of the problems in the church on how to interpret the New Testament position.

Before the verses are considered in more detail it has to be considered how to approach them. In this thesis because the gospels are silent on a subject, it will not be

---

[87] An exception is John Murray who, although seeing that Jesus is addressing men, rejects any gender distinctives in divorce because ' *surely it is necessary to believe that the same rights and liberties are granted to the woman...* ' - see footnote 62 in this thesis. Dr Instone-Brewer sees the Bible as guided purely by contemporary cultural considerations in the matter of gender distinctives in marriage and rejects any consideration of gender in divorce - see reference in footnote 70 of this thesis – and 'Divorce and Remarriage in the Church' Paternoster Press 2003 p119ff. Kostenberger in his recently published and widely acclaimed work acknowledges Instone-Brewer as an authority on divorce in the Bible, but follows his path of gender sameness and assumes that the statements by Jesus in the gospels apply equally to men and women – and so is not convinced by Instone-Brewer's argument about Exodus 21 applying today. Kostenberger 'God Marriage and Family' Crossway 2004. See footnote 25 page 355

Divorce and the Bible

automatically assumed that the relevant Old Testament teaching can no longer be used as a guide. [88] It will be carefully considered when Jesus makes a statement, if that statement is encompassing the whole of divorce teaching, and so all the Old Testament position is superseded, or whether what Jesus says complements what the Old Testament teaches.

In other words it will be asked if when Jesus is silent about something, does it mean that he is removing the Old Testament teaching, that he is changing the status quo?

For example Mark 10:12 records Jesus as saying:-

.......if she divorces her husband and marries another man, she commits adultery.

This is the only statement about divorce from the wife's position in the gospels. Does this mean then that this statement is absolute? That because Jesus does not mention the wife's right of divorce for a husband's unreasonable behaviour he is removing this provision? His silence on the matter removes this long held concession? That a woman can never divorce her husband under any circumstances, ever? Or is Jesus saying that this is a general principle that needed reinforcing in light of the easy divorces being granted in the surrounding Greek and Roman culture?

To treat each pronouncement of Christ as an absolute statement without some reflection would be a very unusual position to take. For example when Jesus says in Matthew 18:19:-

Again, I tell you that if two of you on earth agree about anything you ask for, it will be done for you by my Father in heaven.

---

[88] This 'argument from silence' is considered by Kostenberger 'God Marriage and Family' Crossway 2004 pp242-244. His own review of the literature has failed to show a consideration of this point. This seems to be a remarkable omission which has perhaps led to some of the confusion about divorce teaching today.

Is this to be taken as an absolute pronouncement? Can we really ask anything of God and it will be done for us?

And in Matthew 5:44:-

Love your enemies and pray for those who persecute you.

Does this mean that there is no just war? That when the burglar is raiding your home and then turns to threaten your family you take no direct action? Both these statements – and many others – have to be tackled wisely in the light of other clear Bible teaching. Further, to take the view that if the New Testament does not specifically teach something then any Old Testament teaching has nothing to say to us, is not the historic position of the church.

However, if the view is taken that the New Testament does **not** stand alone, then the application of general principles found in the Old Testament are helpful in reaching a biblical view. For example, just one verse further on from the passage in the Old Testament that talks of a husband's right to divorce, and is the basis of much of what is taught in the New Testament about divorce, we read:-

Do not take a pair of millstones - not even the upper one - as security for a debt, because that would be taking a man's livelihood as security. [89]

This principle, of not removing from a person his means of earning his livelihood when trying to recover a debt, is widely accepted in many societies today. But this is not specifically taught in the New Testament. Similarly, the very next verses to the passage which deals with a wife's right to initiate a divorce, say:-

Anyone who strikes a man and kills him shall surely be put to death. However, if he does not do it intentionally, but God lets it happen, he is to flee to a place I will designate. But if a man schemes and kills another man deliberately, take him away from my altar and put him to death. [90]

---

[89] Deuteronomy 24:6
[90] Exodus 21:12-14

This teaching that differentiates between the different punishments for manslaughter and murder would be difficult to glean from the New Testament alone. But again this teaching is incorporated today in legal systems around the world.

So Old Testament principles are important and can be applied in our Christian era. Old Testament teaching and background, and the mind-set of the first century Jew, are especially important when considering divorce teaching in the gospels in light of the brevity with which the subject is dealt there. That this approach is the right one is indicated by the fact that a considerable portion of Jesus' teaching is in the form of an answer to a question by the Pharisees about the Old Testament teaching.

Jesus' reply to the Pharisees question

The Pharisees asked Jesus about divorce. The real thrust of their question was that they wanted the Lord to express an opinion on Deuteronomy as to who was right – Hillelites with their 'any cause' divorces – or the Shammaites with their teaching that Deuteronomy 24 only allowed divorce for sexual impurity.

The essence of Jesus' reply is in Matthew 19:-

"Moses permitted you to divorce your wives because your hearts were hard. But it was not this way from the beginning. I tell you that anyone who divorces his wife, except for marital unfaithfulness, and marries another woman commits adultery."

The expression *'I tell you'* (or *'but I tell you'* as it is in Matthew 5:32) does not mean that Jesus is correcting or contradicting Moses (it will be remembered that some believe that Moses allowed divorce for trivial reasons) – anymore than when he uses the expression elsewhere in the Sermon on the Mount:-

You have heard that it was said to the people long ago, 'Do not murder, and anyone who murders will be subject to judgment.' But I tell you that anyone who is angry with his brother will be subject to judgement. [91]

Jesus here says that anger is subject to judgement – not instead of murder – but as well as murder. Jesus is emphasising – not changing – the Old Testament. He does not cancel the Old Testament teaching - murder is still wrong!

Furthermore would Jesus be preparing his audience for a change in what Moses taught, when he specifically prefaces his reply about divorce to the Pharisees with the phrase *'Haven't you read..'* ? [92] And in Mark 10:3 when teaching about divorce, with the expression *'What did Moses command you..'*. These phrases are similar to the phrase *'It is written…'* used four times by Jesus earlier in Matthew's gospel when he replied to the devil's temptations in the desert. Jesus in that instance quotes three times from Deuteronomy and once from Psalms – each time reaffirming the teaching there.

And in Matthew 5:18 Jesus says:-

I tell you the truth, until heaven and earth disappear, not the smallest letter, not the least stroke of a pen, will by any means disappear from the Law until everything is accomplished.

Similarly in John 10:35, when Jesus referred to the Old Testament, he said that *'Scripture cannot be broken'*. It is not unreasonable therefore to expect that Jesus was going to base his reply to the Pharisees about divorce on Old Testament teaching. In light of this (and in the view of many commentators), a straightforward reading of the reply Jesus gave is:-

---

[91] Matthew 5: 21,22
[92] Matthew 19:4

- Divorce was not God's intention.

- Moses taught that God allowed divorce because of the Fall.

- The hard hearts belong to us all – believers and unbelievers - we have all shared Adam's fall. Christ removed the penalty for sin for those that are his, but not sin itself, which even Christians have to live with until the day of their final redemption.

- The Deuteronomy passage **is** about sexual impurity.

- Jesus, far from changing this teaching of Moses, confirms it, teaching that *porneia* (sexual impurity – translated marital unfaithfulness in NIV) rather than the specific *moicheia* (adultery) is grounds for divorce - just as Deuteronomy chooses the Hebrew phrase '*erwat dabar* ('indecency' in NIV) rather than the specific *na'aph* (adultery).

And significantly, Jesus in his reply uses the actual wording that the Shammaites used in their teaching.[93] So Jesus was bringing the Pharisees back to their own Scriptures, endorsing the more strict Shammaite teaching, and presenting a consistent position on marriage (and consequently divorce), as a picture of that relationship between God and his people – where God will only divorce his people for 'sexual impurity' - in other words going after other 'gods'. Divorce for sexual impurity (not just adultery) is the clear teaching of Christ in Matthew in complete harmony with the Old Testament. [94]

---

[93] See Instone-Brewer 'Divorce and Remarriage in the Bible' Eerdmans 2002 p102 and Cornes 'Divorce and Remarriage' Eerdmans 1993 p201
[94] For further consideration see Appendix 1: Deuteronomy 24

The missing exception clause

Problems have arisen because although Matthew spells this out clearly in Chapters 5 and 19, a more abbreviated version of what Jesus taught is given in Mark and Luke. Neither of **them** seem to allow any exceptions, instead there appears to be a total ban on divorce and remarriage. In other words while Jesus in Matthew allows husbands to divorce if there has been *'marital unfaithfulness'* – he does not do so in Mark or Luke.

If the exception clause is applied to both Mark and Luke's account it is done so based on an assumption – that we are intended to imply the exception clause in all the divorce statements of Jesus. If this is not done it makes the gospels contradict one another. Most commentators accept that the gospel accounts should be so harmonised by assuming that Mark and Luke simply did not record the exception. It is an eminently reasonable assumption to make and it accords with a widely accepted principle of biblical exegesis.

That this is the correct line to take is reinforced by the fact that the early readers of the gospels would almost certainly have inferred the exception clause for husbands in all Jesus' divorce statements. It has been seen that in New Testament times, one group of Jews believed that Deuteronomy 24 taught that a man could divorce his wife for 'any cause' (the Hillelites), the other group (the Shammaites), thought it taught that divorce was only allowed on the grounds of any sexual impurity by the wife. But **both** believed that a husband could divorce for his wife's sexual impurity. In the social and religious context of AD30 everybody accepted this. Jesus' hearers would have been surprised if Jesus had not allowed divorce for sexual impurity. It was **so** obvious it did not actually need stating. If this seems unlikely to the modern reader – consider this statement:-

"Police say that most crime committed by young people in the community is caused by under-age drinking."

Of course it is alcoholic drinks that are being referred to – everybody today would accept this unsaid assumption.

The surprise and consternation the Lord's disciples express was that sexual impurity was the **only** reason Jesus was giving for a man divorcing his wife. That was not the position of many rabbis – in fact all those that followed Hillel.

What about wives?

Jesus only addresses husbands in this exchange with the Pharisees. Why is this? Because that is what he was asked about – a husband's grounds for divorce. It is not a reasonable assumption that Jesus included wives in his answer – even though virtually all commentators do so. There is no cultural basis to assume this - and it certainly does not fit any accepted rule of biblical exegesis. In Mark 10:12 Jesus speaks for the first (and only) time from the wife's perspective:-

And if she divorces her husband and marries another man, she commits adultery.

Here Jesus makes this separate statement about women at the end of his comments about men and divorce. The fact that he **does** specifically and separately refer to wives here makes it less likely that he was including wives in his teaching about husbands. It can be immediately seen that there is no exception clause. In this verse Jesus is stating a principle, as he did with the men, that women should not divorce. It was never God's intention. Jesus is emphasising God's original plan for marriage.

    Can it then be assumed that Jesus is saying that a woman had no right to divorce her husband on any grounds? We know that there is similarly no exception clause for husbands in Mark or Luke. But nonetheless church tradition, and this thesis, quite reasonably I believe, includes the exception clause for husbands given in Matthew, in the statements recorded about husbands in Mark and Luke. It follows a method of Bible exegesis used by most evangelicals.

Getting the wires crossed

The critical point is that the traditional views go further and include the **husband's** exception clause in this, the only statement by Christ about **wives**; taking Mark 10:12 to mean that a wife can only divorce her husband on the basis of his sexual unfaithfulness.

It is highly unlikely that Jesus' audience would have made this assumption. An assumption of an implied truth must be so obvious that there is no need to state it. So in our day under-age drinking in the earlier example had to refer to alcohol. But it must be remembered that the framework of reference for Jesus' audience is the Old Testament Scriptures – there is as yet no New Testament. A wife knew that her husband could divorce her if she went with another man – another 'Christ' - as that would be adultery. But to make the grounds for divorce for husbands and wives the same would mean a husband would be guilty of adultery against his own first wife if he took a second wife. This would in the minds of Jesus' hearers invalidate the plural marriages of some of the greatest Old Testament saints. These marriages were considered valid at that time - if they were not so it would mean that any child born to them would be illegitimate.

Deuteronomy 23:2 says:

No one born of a forbidden marriage nor any of his descendants may enter the assembly of the LORD, even down to the tenth generation.

It has been seen that Exodus 21 permitted a wife to divorce her husband if he took another wife – not because that second marriage was sinful, but in so doing he was not fulfilling her expectations of her own marriage. But a wife was not allowed to take a second husband. In contrast Jacob (Israel) had four wives – and only six of his sons were from Leah, his first wife, but all his twelve sons formed the earthly Israel. Indeed the Lord himself is recorded in Matthew Chapter 1 as legitimately descended from Solomon,

Divorce and the Bible

the son of David and Bathsheba – probably David's eighth wife. [95]

To make the grounds for divorce gender neutral is a radical new teaching of enormous theological, legal and practical import that would have to be stated – not left as an unsaid implication so obvious that it did not need saying. It is a teaching that would leave many of the Old Testament saints adulterers, half of Israel illegitimate, and casts doubt on the Lord's own ancestry. Even if the reader believes that the New Testament (completed some decades later) teaches gender neutral divorce elsewhere, it still could not be left as an unsaid implication in this one brief aside to the Pharisees. (See Appendix 3 for a fuller consideration of Mark 10:12).

The correct assumption

In light of this - is it not wiser to consider that the exception clause for **wives** should be assumed in Christ's statement about **wives**? That this exception clause was so well known that Jesus did not have to say it every time he made a general statement? Life would be impossible if every time we made a general statement every exception would have to be mentioned. The right of a wife to divorce on the grounds of her husband's unreasonable behaviour was the Jewish understanding of the Old Testament. The Shammaites and Hillelites were united on it. [96] Jesus had effectively endorsed the Shammaite position on divorce for men by the precise wording of his exception clause in the gospels when he was speaking about husbands - it was the actual Shammaite wording he used.

If Jesus had disagreed with the other Shammaite divorce teaching that was widely known and accepted,

---

[95] The taking of more than one wife – polygamy – or more strictly polygyny – was often Old Testament practice. Like slavery it is never forbidden – but rather hedged about with legislation such as Exodus 21. The New Testament does not unequivocally address either, but the church has seen that the whole New Testament ethos militates against both.

[96] See Instone-Brewer 'Divorce and Remarriage in the Bible' Eerdmans 2002 p102

that a wife could initiate a divorce based on a husband's unreasonable behaviour, it would have been logical, indeed imperative you would have thought, to distance himself from that position. He did not.

It is again eminently reasonable to assume, as with husbands, that the wives' exception clause was not specifically referred to by Jesus in this context because it was so well known. Although it has to be accepted that unlike his comments about husbands, Jesus is never recorded as mentioning the wife's basis for divorce elsewhere in the gospels.

But it must be borne in mind Jesus was not giving teaching about wives, he was not asked about them – his comment is an aside. And there are many things Jesus did not specifically teach about that are accepted as applicable to Christians today. He did not speak on manslaughter, or the right of a widow to remarry. Instead he tended to speak on controversial issues; areas where there were misunderstandings that had to be corrected. He had to correct misconceptions about worship, who our neighbour was, the nature of the kingdom, what true faith was, the Sabbath day and so on.

And the New Testament is not silent about a wife's rightful expectations of her husband. Ephesians 5 repeats the husband's obligations contained in Exodus 21 and it will be seen that 1 Corinthians 7 reflects the same language in its descriptions of marital obligations.

So the issue is not:-

- **Does a Christian husband have the obligations imposed on him contained in Exodus 21?**

But rather:-

- **Does a wife have a right to divorce her husband, as she had up until the time of Christ, if he fails in his duties?**

When asked about Deuteronomy 24 Jesus did not repeal the right of a man to divorce his wife if she was involved in sexual immorality. Instead he repeated the Deuteronomy teaching. It defies logic and any sound basis of exegesis, if when restating the husband's right to divorce, it is considered Jesus simultaneously withdrew the wife's right so to do (as outlined in Exodus 21), and do so by a silent implication.

Furthermore Exodus 21, like Deuteronomy 24, contains teaching about divorce that is totally consistent with the notion that marriage (and divorce) is a picture of the great redemptive theme of the Bible. In the unlikely event that this Exodus teaching was being radically changed so that there was now a **less** clear picture of a believer's relationship with their Saviour, would Jesus have not said so? And why would Jesus preface this divorce statement when he mentions wives with - *'what did Moses command you?'* – implying he was going to base his reply on the Pentateuch. Those that believe Jesus overturned a clear Old Testament teaching that was widely accepted in his day have an impossible exegetical position to rely on.

The Lord's statement about wives recorded by Mark in his gospel is an aside; he was stating a general principle, not giving his full teaching on wives and divorce. He was not reversing an historic Old Testament teaching – anymore than he was when he addressed husbands.

Some further questions addressed:-

- **Are you saying a woman cannot divorce her husband for his sexual unfaithfulness?**

Not at all. In fact this is the very situation in Exodus 21. Her husband has taken another wife – the first wife can go. She could divorce him for that - just as she could if any of her expectations of him in his role were not met. The decision is hers. (But as has been seen – taking a second wife was not considered a sexual sin in Old Testament Israel).

- **What about eunuchs and the kingdom of God?**

The disciples said to him, "If this is the situation between a husband and wife, it is better not to marry." Jesus replied,

"Not everyone can accept this word, but only those to whom it has been given. For some are eunuchs because they were born that way; others were made that way by men; and others have renounced marriage because of the kingdom of heaven. The one who can accept this should accept it." [97]

Having been told that a man can only divorce his wife for her sexual immorality the disciples express some consternation. It does seem that the Pharisees at the time had largely adopted the Hillel position which made divorce for men easy. Jesus goes on to say that it is not compulsory to marry – you can be like a eunuch! In other words it is possible to live a life with no sexual expression. This had not been an option for a Jewish man. Rabbinical teaching was that a man must marry to fulfil the duties of Genesis 1:28 where the first couple are commanded to *'be fruitful and increase in number'.*

Jesus is making the same point that Paul makes later – that singleness in the Christian life is an acceptable option before God. Indeed some might opt for that life style for the sake of the kingdom, more to serve their Saviour. And in the context here Jesus is saying that if you cannot accept the rules of marriage – do not get married.

- **Why didn't Jesus mention this exception clause for wives?**

Jesus is not recorded as being asked about the position of women. Jesus was saying to both the men and the women that the general rule is **no** divorce. God hates it. It was not his original intention. Also it must be accepted that not everything Jesus said is recorded in the gospels. And quite probably Jesus did not teach about every subject. It is logical that when he was clarifying something that was contentious (like a husband's grounds for divorce), or teaching something new (like him being raised from the dead after three days), that **that** is recorded. We do not

---

[97] Matthew 19:10-12

read that he said incest or rape was wrong. These teachings were so generally accepted that there was no point in him saying it, or if he did, of the gospel writers recording it. If everything he actually said and did was recorded the Bible would be a very big book indeed. Judaism was united in its teaching on Exodus 21; it was biblical, clear and accepted. There was no reason why Jesus would mention it.

- **It is still difficult to believe that this key exception clause was left unsaid**

It is accepted among evangelicals that in the synoptic gospels, when considering one gospel, some clarification might have to be sought from the other gospels. The wife's exception clause is not in another gospel, but it is in the Bible – in Exodus. For many years the church misinterpreted and misapplied Leviticus 18:16 because they did not see a hidden implication that must have been obvious at the time it was written (see Chapter 8). And it has been seen in our modern world how key pieces of information can be left out of statements because they **are** so widely accepted.

- **What is the significance of the point being made?**

Is it really so important to establish that Jesus did not change the Old Testament teaching and instead retained the different grounds for divorce for husbands and wives? In some ways this does seem academic. As was said earlier it was always possible for a woman to divorce her husband for **any** sexual sin if she so chooses. But if a new 'rule' is made here, and done so simply on the basis of harmonising Jesus' teaching with modern expectations of gender equality, then the gender distinctives in the grounds for divorce start to crumble. Not only is the important picture of Christ and the church lost, it increases the vulnerability of women, in these two ways:-

Either:-

- Exodus 21 is not accepted as a basis for divorce today. The traditional teaching is maintained in that a man and woman have the same rules for divorce - that is based on sexual sins only. With such teaching a wife can be subject to an abusive uncaring husband and has no legitimate way out of the marriage except on grounds based on her husband's sexual unfaithfulness.

Or:-

- Exodus 21 is accepted as a basis for divorce, but the traditional view of 'sameness' in the divorce rules is retained.[98] Then it follows a man can divorce his wife for her failure to provide for him. This is very difficult to define. A woman as a consequence loses her security in the marriage.

This second position is in effect the position that pertains today in the statute law in England with 'no fault' divorce. If one partner wants to initiate a divorce the other eventually has to agree without there being any need to establish a cause.

- **Isn't all this difficult to grasp?**

For many the paradigm with which they come to the subject is the traditional teaching of the church today – that is - when Jesus spoke to men he included women, and that we are to assume the exception clause for women is the same as for men – divorce only for sexual impurity. But in that New Testament era everybody in the community was clear about a husband's responsibilities, everybody accepted them, and that a wife could divorce her husband

---

[98] Instone-Brewer takes this view

if he did not fulfil them. [99] It was also accepted that a man could divorce his wife for sexual unfaithfulness. However a certain group was teaching that a man had similar 'leeway' as his wife – that there were all sorts of reasons he could divorce his wife. It was the 'cause celebre' of the day. People were talking about it – could a man really divorce his wife for 'any cause'?

The 'any cause' divorce **was** popular - it was far more discreet. It seems Joseph was going to opt for an 'any cause' divorce with Mary, there would be no accusation, no possibility of stoning for adultery.[100] Understandably it was popular among husbands, and some wives as well. It was no surprise therefore that the Pharisees came to Jesus with a question about it. It has been seen that the Hillelites wanted the restricted grounds for divorce for men expanding to include virtually anything the husband did not like about his wife. They wanted divorce for 'any cause'. This is the question that was asked Jesus. Everybody accepted – including the Hillelites - that the wife's grounds for divorce were different from that of the husband.

Re-read the gospel accounts with that perspective – and I believe they are clear. There is no basis for the traditional views saying that Jesus swept away all the Old Testament teaching and replaced it with rules that gave new restricted grounds for a wife's divorce based on gender equality – for which can be read gender 'sameness'. And all of this by implication – not in any recorded statement.

---

[99] '*Even before the announcement of the Se'elim 'get' there is a consensus that women could, under many circumstances, gain a divorce from their husbands within first-century Palestinian Judaism. Since its publication there are few who would argue this consensus.. The internal evidence of the Mishnah suggests that there were several cases where women brought appeals for divorce to rabbinic courts in or before the first century, based on the obligations of Exodus 21:10-11.*' Instone-Brewer 'Divorce and Remarriage in the Bible' Eerdmans 2002 p90ff

[100] Matthew1:19 ' *Because Joseph her husband was a righteous man and did not want to expose her to public disgrace, he had in mind to divorce her quietly*'

Jesus and Divorce

An illustration

Originally the motorway system in the UK was derestricted. Only in 1964 was the new national speed limit of 70mph introduced. This is not a uniform limit. Some sections of the motorway have permanent speed limits of 50mph, some have varying limits depending on traffic flow or road works, and of course emergency service vehicles on call do not have any such restriction. The guidelines for all of this are outlined in the Department of Transport's Highway Code. There is however a pressure group in the UK trying to get the speed limit raised on the motorway system to 80mph. They accept that the urban speed limit should stay at 30 mph. Imagine if the Minister for Transport is asked about the motorway limit in a television interview. The Minister is not asked about the urban limit – but includes it in his reply.

His reply:-

"Haven't you read the Highway Code? It was not so in the beginning, but I tell you - the limit now is 70mph and is going to stay. The urban speed limit also remains the same."

Remember what Jesus told the Pharisees in answer to their question about husbands?

Haven't you read ….at the beginning of creation God 'made them male and female'….[before the Fall there was no divorce].

But I tell you …….anyone who divorces his wife and marries another woman commits adultery against her. And if she divorces her husband and marries another man, she commits adultery.

Now imagine two different newspapers reporting the Minister's comment the next day:-

Newspaper A

Minister reiterates the principle of 70 mph speed limit on the UK motorway network, and reminds viewers of the urban speed limit. It is presumed the exceptions outlined in the Highway Code still apply.

Newspaper B

Minister scraps his own department's Highway Code guidelines and removes all differential speed limits on the motorway system replacing them with a uniform 70mph. In addition he harmonises the urban speed limit with that of the motorway on the basis of fairness.

Which is the more reasonable interpretation of the Minister's comments? No matter how it is presented the latter is how many of the traditional views interpret the divorce statements of Christ in the gospels. Based on his brief comments they tell us that (uniquely) the Old Testament is swept aside and gender distinctives lost. But Jesus did not revoke the Old Testament position; he did not change the accepted teaching. He brought the Pharisees back to their own Scriptures and clarified the position that men could only divorce their wives for sexual impurity. He was not asked the position of women so he did not address the subject of their grounds for divorce.

- **Let's be clear**

There is a doctrine called the perspicuity of Scripture. This means that on the key matters that relate to our redemption the Bible is clear. The Westminster Confession says:-

All things in Scripture are not alike plain in themselves, nor alike clear unto all: yet those things which are necessary to be known, believed, and observed for salvation are so clearly propounded, and opened in some place of Scripture or other, that not only the learned, but the unlearned, in a due use of the ordinary means, may attain unto a sufficient understanding of them.

It has to be accepted that on some matters the Bible is less obviously straightforward. We should not be surprised that this includes divorce, in that divorce has the potential in and of itself to be quite a complex subject. But the straightforward statements of Jesus have been made more complex by the traditional views than they actually are. The complexity some have seen in the gospels is not due primarily to difficulties in what is actually recorded in Scripture - it has been more to do with the paradigm with which the subject has been approached. The traditional model does not sit well with many of the texts, so a tortuous and often confusing exegesis has to be attempted to make them fit.

To return to our jigsaw analogy, the traditional views are pressing pieces into place that do not fit well. The resulting picture is not consistent with any systematic approach to biblical theology – and what is more it is found that their nearly completed jigsaw does not say on what grounds a woman can divorce. They believe no teaching for this is to be found – so a new jigsaw piece is made – '*only a husband's sexual unfaithfulness*'.

The traditional views see that:-

- When Jesus addresses the issue in Deuteronomy 24 he is asked about, in his reply he is cancelling all the Old Testament teaching on divorce, including passages such as Exodus 21.

- When Jesus is asked about men and specifically says he is talking about men he means women as well.

- All the teaching about divorce concerning men can be applied to women as well, not on scriptural grounds, but on the grounds of fairness.

- When Jesus says (Mark 10:12) that women should **not** divorce their husbands he is really saying that for the first time women **could** divorce their husbands. (The traditional views to date have largely assumed a wife could not divorce her husband in Old Testament Israel).

- Implied statements are assumed in the sayings of Jesus that are not found anywhere in the Bible – specifically that a woman's only grounds for divorce are her husband's sexual impurity.

- Jesus introduced a fundamental discontinuity between the Testaments on the subject of divorce that is not seen in any other area.

In contrast this thesis maintains that:-

- When Jesus addresses the question the Pharisees put to him about Deuteronomy 24, that is what he is referring to, and he does not change the position on the wider issues of divorce.

- When Jesus is asked about men and divorce and he specifically says in his reply that he is talking about men, that he really does mean men.

- Jesus was not harmonising the husband's and wife's position on the grounds of fairness. The Old Testament position where women did have different (and more 'generous') grounds for divorce remained the same.

- An implication in the gospel statements is only included when it is found in the Bible.

- When Jesus talks about women and divorce (Mark 10:12) he does not really mean the opposite of what he actually says.

- Jesus did not introduce a radical discontinuity between the Testaments in his teaching on divorce.

Jesus and Divorce

Some initial conclusions

Jesus in these gospel statements is simply taking the Pharisees back to Scripture and making these points:-

- Marriage was always intended to be lifelong.

- God did not initiate divorce – it came into the nation and legislation for it was given because of the 'hardness of their hearts'.

- The rules are clear; for the women - they can divorce if their husband's behaviour is unreasonable. Jesus did not teach about this because it was not in dispute.

- For the men - divorce is only permissible if the wife is sexually impure. Why did Jesus teach about this? Because it was in dispute and he was specifically asked about it.

Christ and the church

The New Testament expands on the theme of God being the bridegroom of Israel by teaching us that the church is Christ's bride. Jesus keeps this picture intact in his teaching about divorce in the exchange with the Pharisees recorded for us in the gospels. The man is to be like Christ keeping hold of the church through all her difficulties. The woman is a 'type' of believer, knowing that her husband, her 'Christ' will never let her go. Only if she repudiates him by going with another is he permitted to divorce her. If she takes another husband, another 'god', she cannot come back - as Deuteronomy 24 tells us.

Surely here is seen the outworking of a great gospel truth:-

Here is a trustworthy saying:
If we died with him, we will also live with him;
if we endure, we will also reign with him.
If we disown him, he will also disown us;

Divorce and the Bible

*if we are faithless, he will remain faithful,
for he cannot disown himself* [101]

And a great gospel warning:-

Today, if you hear his voice, do not harden your hearts as you did in the rebellion, during the time of testing in the desert, where your fathers tested and tried me and for forty years saw what I did. That is why I was angry with that generation, and I said, 'Their hearts are always going astray, and they have not known my ways.' So I declared on oath in my anger, 'They shall never enter my rest.' See to it, brothers, that none of you has a sinful, unbelieving heart that turns away from the living God. [102]

This perspective of marriage and divorce is crucially lost in all the traditional views. Because commentators are so keen to see 'equal rights' for women they put women in the same position as men. This means that women can divorce only for sexual unfaithfulness, but for no other reason. Not only then is the picture of Christ and the church lost but women become vulnerable to an abusive uncaring husband and a lifetime of misery.

Many who write books on divorce have pastoral responsibilities and recognise the problem of confining the grounds for divorce to sexual unfaithfulness only. So after rehearsing a traditional view they often start to introduce other grounds (not based on any exegesis of the texts) that they would allow a wife (and it is usually the wife) to divorce their husband.[103] Not wishing to criticise this expression of compassion in a field where so often compassion seems to be in short supply, but to proceed on a pastorally pragmatic basis surely defeats the object of trying to arrive at a consistent exposition of the texts.

---

[101] 2 Timothy 2:11-13
[102] Hebrews 3:7-12
[103] For example Keener '.. and marries another' Hendrickson 1991 Chapter 8 and Heth in 'Divorce and Remarriage' IVP 1990 p59

Jesus and Divorce

With so many difficulties raised by the traditional teaching both exegetically and practically - why is it so widespread? Those writers that realise they are building a doctrine on a teaching not found in the Bible usually justify this by saying that 'gender equality must be presumed'. But there is and always was 'equality'; what is really meant is 'sameness'. Sameness was not ever in God's plan for men and women. Together as male and female they are in his image.[104] Different yet complementary. Of course once you have 'sameness' you lose the picture of Christ and the church. Some of these same writers who introduce this concept of 'equality' into the grounds for divorce, often then go on to deny male headship – a logical step. [105] Chapter 10 will consider how this thesis can be applied in pastoral situations.

Key Points

- **The teaching of the Old Testament and the New Testament is consistent**

- **Jesus' general statements about divorce are just that – statements of general principle**

- **Jesus did not cancel the Old Testament concessions on divorce – he clarified those he was asked about**

---

[104] Genesis 1:27
[105] Particularly striking in this is Instone-Brewer in 'Divorce an Remarriage in the Church' p119ff

7 Paul and Divorce

Paul's teaching about divorce is contained in 1 Corinthians 7. At first sight it is a complicated chapter. Paul quickly covers many aspects of marriage, divorce and the single state. While the passage should not be approached with pre-conceived ideas about what Paul must say – it would be surprising if he did not hold these five principles:-

1. **Marriage is good**
2. **Singleness is good**
3. **Marriage is to be life long - divorce is not what God intended**
4. **Divorce is permissible**
5. **Marriage is a picture of God's relationship to his church and divorce was allowed when this picture was broken**

Why? Because this is what the Old and New Testaments teach elsewhere.

Paul's five clear principles

1 Marriage is good

Now for the matters you wrote about: It is good for a man not to marry. But since there is so much immorality, each man should have his own wife, and each woman her own husband. The husband should fulfil his marital duty to his wife, and likewise the wife to her husband. The wife's body does not belong to her alone but also to her husband. In the same way, the husband's body does not belong to him alone but also to his wife. Do not deprive each other except by mutual consent and for a time, so that you may devote yourselves to prayer. Then come together again so that Satan will not tempt you because of your lack of self-control. I say this as a concession, not as a command. I wish that all men were as I am. But each man has his own gift from God; one has this gift, another has that. Now to the unmarried and the widows I say: It is good for them to stay unmarried, as I am. But if they cannot control themselves, they should marry, for it is better to marry than to burn with passion (v1-9)

'It is good for a man not to marry'. [106] This does not sound like a ringing endorsement of marriage and I am inclined to agree with the view outlined in the footnote. But it must be remembered that what Paul is saying here is not his whole teaching on marriage for which, as is seen elsewhere, he has an exalted view. He is simply here dealing with specific issues. If the NIV is followed, Paul is saying that it is alright not to marry. But he then goes on to say that sexual relations within marriage are ordained by God, that marriage is God given.

2 Singleness is good

'I wish that all men were as I am' (v 7) - that is single. Paul thought the single state was good. This was an unusual statement to make at the time because all Jewish men saw it as their duty to marry. Paul does not place that duty on Christians, neither as we have seen did Jesus.

3 Marriage is to be lifelong

- **divorce is not what God intended**

To the married I give this command (not I, but the Lord): A wife must not separate from her husband ....And a husband must not divorce his wife (v10..11)

Paul states this general principle (as Jesus did in Mark and Luke) and repeats it at the end of the chapter addressing himself specifically to the woman:-

---

[106] Some hold that in v1 Paul is quoting something the Corinthians were saying – as it is translated in the King James Version - that it is *'good for a man not to touch a woman'*, implying that it is more spiritual to abstain from any sexual expression even within marriage. The Corinthians it seems were already adopting an ascetic approach. Paul is disagreeing with that position.

A woman is bound to her husband as long as he lives. But if her husband dies, she is free to marry anyone she wishes, but he must belong to the Lord. In my judgment, she is happier if she stays as she is--and I think that I too have the Spirit of God. (v39, 40)

But then he says:

But if she does [separate], she must remain unmarried or else be reconciled to her husband. (v11)

So it can be seen that Paul **was** dealing in general principles because immediately he admits that a wife might indeed 'separate' from her husband. Although here Paul says that any such separation (not divorce) should be temporary.

- **no divorce even for mixed marriages**

To the rest I say this (I, not the Lord): If any brother has a wife who is not a believer and she is willing to live with him, he must not divorce her. And if a woman has a husband who is not a believer and he is willing to live with her, she must not divorce him. (v12,13)

Paul teaches something new (hence in v12 'I, not the Lord'). What new thing is this? Those who hold the traditional views jump forward to verse 15 and say it is that an unbelieving spouse can be divorced (or allowed to separate) if they desert. But it is in this very paragraph v12-14 that the new teaching is contained. Paul goes straight to his point - it is in fact virtually the opposite of what the traditional views teach - *'If any brother has a wife who is not a believer... he must not divorce her'*. In other words no divorce even for 'mixed' marriages! Paul knew this would run counter to Jewish sensibilities of the day. He then says why he teaches this.....

- **because mixed marriages are sanctified marriages**

For the unbelieving husband has been sanctified through

his wife, and the unbelieving wife has been sanctified through her believing husband. Otherwise your children would be unclean, but as it is, they are holy.(v14)

Mixed marriages are to be considered 'sanctified' marriages and the children are 'holy'. Such marriages in the Jewish nation had been forbidden.[107] The Jews had been repeatedly taught not to marry outside the faith – to keep the nation pure. Old Testament Israel had a propensity to adopt the pagan practices of surrounding nations. This was a particular hazard when Jewish people married non-Jews – especially for Jewish men who took non-Jewish wives; here the wife's influence in the home on any children could lead to the loss of the distinctives of the Jewish faith. Some would go further and say that children of Old Testament non-Jewish wives were 'unclean' or 'illegitimate'.[108] Paul says they are sanctified. [109]

So Paul gives distinctive New Testament teaching. He does not advocate a Christian marrying an unbeliever – far from it – but he does say in the Christian home an unbelieving spouse benefits from Christian influence - not that the unbeliever 'pollutes' the family. And the children? Rather than being illegitimate they would be considered holy.

---

[107] Deuteronomy 7:2-4
[108] Easton's Bible Dictionary says this about the meaning of 'illegitimate' :
In the Old Testament the rendering of the Hebrew word 'mamzer', means 'polluted'. In Deut. 23:2, it occurs in the ordinary sense of illegitimate offspring. In Zech. 9:6, the word is used in the sense of foreigner. From the history of Jephthah we learn that there were bastard offspring among the Jews (Judges 11:1-7).
[109] The Old Testament prohibition on mixed marriages referred to marrying a non-Jew – it was not prohibiting marrying a (Jewish) unbeliever. It was the purity of the Jewish nation that was at stake. Paul's teaching that marriage with an unbeliever is a sanctified marriage is new – but even here we do not see a reversal of Old Testament teaching - those principles referred to the Jewish people as a nation. Paul does not address that issue – he is addressing the church era.

- **so in mixed marriages the same rules apply**

The conventional wisdom is that Jesus only addressed the marriages of believers, so Paul has to give separate rules for mixed marriages.[110] But this is not so. Jesus addressed the subject of marriage in the context of the Jewish situation he was asked about, and in so doing he appealed to the creation ordinance of marriage in Genesis 1:27 and 2:24 - it is an ordinance that embraces **all** marriages - Jewish, Christian or 'mixed'; marriages of other religions or no religion. So there can be no new divorce rules - no new exceptions. That Jesus spoke to all marriages is a point made by many when the gospel statements about marriage are being considered in isolation to any divorce teaching. Paul had to clarify that in the church age the concept of a mixed marriage had changed and (probably addressing Jewish Christians in particular) such couples were not to seek new grounds for divorce.

4 Divorce is permissible

But if the unbeliever leaves, let him do so. A believing man or woman is not bound in such circumstances; God has called us to live in peace. How do you know, wife, whether you will save your husband? Or, how do you know, husband, whether you will save your wife? (v15,16)

Like Jesus, Paul has dealt with general principles but then finally says - in the context of mixed marriages - that if your spouse leaves, you can let them go. Why does Paul mention this now? Because mixed marriages are vulnerable marriages. Paul has already addressed the believers in a mixed marriage in v12-14 – they are not to initiate a divorce based on the belief of their partner. But he realises that the unbelieving partner might unilaterally decide to leave. They

---

[110] For example Jay Adams 'Marriage, Divorce, and Remarriage in the Bible' Zondervan 1980 p38

would not feel bound by any apostle's plea – or even any command of the Lord. This is the situation Paul addresses, and in so doing he does not teach new material, but instead applies the principles from Exodus 21 to desertion. There the teaching is clear – if a wife wants to go the husband is to let her – she has divorced him. If a husband deserts, by definition he is not providing for his wife, and she is free to divorce him.

Most who hold to the traditional views believe that because Paul talks about desertion in this context it only applies in this context. It is rather like setting out on a car journey and saying to your travelling companions – I have had some trouble with that tyre – it must have a slow puncture. Then one of the group says – if it goes down we will have to change it. Of course it is not intended to mean that if another tyre goes down that that one will not be changed.

This is Paul's point about mixed marriages - they are by their nature vulnerable. Desertion can be treated as a divorce initiated by the deserting partner – more likely to happen if they are an unbeliever. The key point is the desertion – a potential consequence of a mixed marriage - not the belief of the partner.

- **But does desertion mean divorce?**

If the (unbelieving) spouse leaves the believer is 'not bound'. But what does this mean? Some think when Paul says believers in this situation are 'not bound', that he means they are not bound to hold the marriage together, they are not bound to live with the person. They can separate. But it is very difficult to see this could be the meaning on simply logistical grounds. If a spouse leaves there is little that can be done about it!

Another argument is that Paul in the phrase 'not bound' uses a different verb to the verb normally used to refer to marriage, so he is not saying the marriage is ended when he says you are not bound. But if Paul had used the same verb, he would have been saying that if the unbelieving spouse leaves, you are 'not married' – implying that the mixed marriage was never a valid

Divorce and the Bible

marriage. [111] Further when Paul uses the phrase 'not bound', he is using the terminology of virtually every divorce certificate in contemporary Jewish society that specifically meant that such a deserted person was free to divorce and remarry. [112] Is this probable if that was the very meaning he wanted to avoid? In contemporary society (Rome in particular) separation and remarriage was rife. Couples separated simply because they wanted to make a new liaison. There was no concept of long-term separation being a different state from that of being divorced.[113] Surely Paul would have had to make himself more clear to his readers if he meant something else. The Exodus 21 phrase 'to go free' meant that a wife was free to remarry; not *agunah* – not bound. [114]

5 Marriage is a picture of God's relationship to his church and divorce was allowed when this picture was broken

1 Corinthians 7 maintains the picture of Christ and the church. This might not be immediately apparent, but when Paul's words are looked at in this light, it can be seen that he is faithful to this picture, and indeed to the teaching of Exodus 21. Paul never says to a husband he can initiate a divorce against his wife for a new reason - desertion. Why not? Because Jesus had said clearly that the only reason a husband can initiate a divorce against his wife is for her sexual impurity. But Paul **is** saying that if a wife deserts her husband he can treat the desertion as if she has divorced him. The Bible does not teach that there is such a thing as a long term 'separated but still married' state as there might be in UK law. And a wife can treat her husband's desertion as his unreasonable behaviour – and so divorce him.

---

[111] See Edgar 'Divorce and Remarriage' Inter Varsity Press 1990 p189ff.
[112] Instone-Brewer 'Divorce and Remarriage in the Bible' Eerdmans 2002 p202
[113] Instone-Brewer 'Divorce and Remarriage in the Bible' Eerdmans 2002 p190. See also Stephen Clark 'Putting Asunder...' Bryntirion Press 1999 pp 137-143 for the contemporary social background to Paul's letter.
[114] See Appendix 5: Agunah

Eight points of clarification

1 The Jewish perspective on mixed marriages

Even though the predominant influence from the surrounding culture in the Corinthian church would have been Hellenistic, any Jewish male converts in particular might have assumed they should, or at least could, separate from their unbelieving wife as this was the specific instruction of Ezra when the Jews returned from exile. [115] There were many Jewish perspectives in the New Testament church that Paul had to deal with in his ministry that we read of elsewhere in his letters. Paul had to cover this point in case any had in their minds brought this teaching into the church context.

2 Paul teaches that desertion is divorce

If your unbelieving wife leaves you, Paul says let them go. This is an application of the Exodus 21 teaching. There the man is to let his wife go if she so chooses. She is not to be held by force, she is to 'go free' – that is not bound. Neither should the Christian husband bind his wife to himself in this New Testament era. As has been seen the Bible does not teach a double standard. There are not separate rules for believers and unbelievers. The personal faith of the wife has no bearing on the rules - the marriage is over even if a believing wife leaves. If your unbelieving husband leaves you, then by definition he is not providing for you – and Exodus 21 clearly comes into play; you are free to divorce him, you are to go free, not bound, and are free to remarry.

The faith of the deserting partner is not the relevant point. A Christian husband can fail to provide just as effectively as an unbeliever if he has a mind so to do. Paul's teaching - allowing the deserted partner to treat the desertion as a divorce initiated against them - is entirely

---

[115] Ezra 10

consistent with the Old Testament position. Paul is not introducing a new rule, he is simply applying an existing teaching to the specific situation of a mixed marriage.

3 Is it really not different for the believing couple?

When Paul is talking about mixed marriages in his letter we cannot assume that he is ruling out the possibility of desertion by a believer, or that if such a thing happened a different set of rules would apply. His emphasis has been that the same rules apply to both groups. Just because he does not cover that particular situation here, it is a strange exegesis that assumes different rules then apply, unless these different rules can be found elsewhere. And they are not to be found. Also Paul's teaching here cannot be taken in isolation. He is not writing a thesis on divorce as if there is no other teaching available. The Old Testament position was clear and Jesus had already repeated the grounds for a divorce initiated by a husband outlined in Deuteronomy 24.

This is Paul's starting point. Everything Paul says falls into place with Exodus 21, Deuteronomy 24 and the Lord's statements in the gospels. Even when Paul in his letters preserved for us in the Bible is at his most radical, he never stands Old Testament principles on their head. Instead he reinforces them, showing the true spiritual nature of the old covenant. [116] The teaching of Paul is not a new departure, it is not the 'Pauline exception' reserved for unbelievers. It is true he does not address the believing couple on the specific issue of desertion or failure to provide, but that was not his subject. He does not address here either the issue of a believing (or unbelieving) wife being sexually immoral; that is dealt with in the gospels.

There are not multiple biblical standards for marriage in the world based on belief systems; although of course only those that accept the Lordship of Christ will look to abide by the biblical standard. It is reckless to advise unbelievers

---

[116] For example circumcision, and the true nature of Jewishness – Romans 2.

that God holds non-Christians to a lesser standard of sexual conduct inside or outside of marriage. So it is not correct to say that Jesus only gave the rules for a marriage where both partners were believers – therefore Paul has to now give new rules for this 'new' situation.

If Paul was going to introduce different rules you would expect him to emphasise the difference by saying what it was. But this is not at all the thrust of Paul's argument; instead he repeats the same rules for this other group. Paul applies his general principle of no divorce to a 'mixed' marriage.

The teaching of the traditional views when they come to 1 Corinthians 7 is that there **are** different rules for each partner within the same marriage. This leads to the anomalous position that when, for example, a believing wife is deserted by a husband who is a believer, she is told she cannot re-marry. If her husband is an unbeliever – she can. In other words a wife's future life pattern is determined by the ongoing profession of an absent husband.

4 Exodus 21 applied

Exodus 21 shows that a wife in Israel could take the initiative and divorce – and the husband should let her go. The position for Christians is no different. Exodus 21 does not say a husband can initiate a divorce, but he is to accept a divorce initiated by his wife. It would be unreasonable to argue from silence that Paul was abrogating Exodus 21 when he uses those very principles in his argument. It cannot be assumed that Paul is ruling out the possibility of desertion by a believer – or that if such a thing happened a different set of rules applied. There is no good reason to restrict the application of the principles of Exodus 21 to mixed marriages simply because that is Paul's purpose here in 1 Corinthians 7.

For all these reasons it is more reasonable to assume that Paul's teaching endorses the Exodus 21 position for both believers and unbelievers. Paul does **not** say - *if you are deserted by your spouse **and** they are an unbeliever .. then...* The conditional 'if' in Paul's actual statement relates to the desertion, not primarily to their status as an unbeliever.

5 Paul's exhortation

The traditional views say that Jesus taught that a wife could divorce her husband only for his sexual unfaithfulness – but now Paul is going to introduce a new additional concession. But is it not more likely the newly converted wife thought she might already have grounds to divorce her unbelieving husband – and Paul far from making a concession – looks to discourage her from so doing with his exhortation? She was entitled in Exodus 21 to material and emotional support – how could an unbelieving husband fulfil that duty? Surely her new found faith meant that she should seek a new, Christian husband, to fulfil those needs?

To paraphrase Paul, he says to the Christian wife:-

'I now appeal to you as an apostle not to divorce your husband simply because he is an unbeliever.'

It is no coincidence that in so doing the actual language he uses is a close parallel to the Exodus 21 passage.[117]

So Paul appeals to:

- Christian husbands not to divorce unbelieving wives. They had a right to divorce for a wife's sexual immorality – but they might have thought that Ezra's example gave them another cause for divorce.

- Christian wives not to divorce their unbelieving husbands. They might have thought having a non-Christian husband could put them in an unreasonable situation, giving them the divorce rights of Exodus 21. Interestingly Paul would not have had to make

---

[117] Instone-Brewer 'Divorce and Remarriage in the Bible' Eerdmans 2002 p193

Paul and Divorce

this plea if Jesus had cancelled the wife's right to divorce for a husband's unreasonable behaviour in Mark 10:12.

6   What about 'stay as you are'?

In the verses 17 to 24 Paul is saying do not seek a change in your circumstance simply because you have become a Christian. (Again one should allow here an implied truth. If God calls you to faith in Christ while you are a professional burglar obviously you should change jobs.) He then applies that principle to the married and single state in verses 25-38. Paul is not forbidding marriage or divorce; he is dealing with general principles.

7   What about 1 Corinthians 7:39?

A woman is bound to her husband as long as he lives. But if her husband dies, she is free to marry anyone she wishes, but he must belong to the Lord.

Here Paul summarises what he is saying by repeating his principle - *'she is bound to her husband as long as he lives'*. He has told us in what situations she is not bound.

8   What about Romans 7:1-3?

Do you not know, brothers--for I am speaking to men who know the law--that the law has authority over a man only as long as he lives? For example, by law a married woman is bound to her husband as long as he is alive, but if her husband dies, she is released from the law of marriage. So then, if she marries another man while her husband is still alive, she is called an adulteress. But if her husband dies, she is released from that law and is not an adulteress, even though she marries another man

Paul is not talking about divorce here - he is talking about the law. He uses the nature of marriage as an illustration of the law. He is talking about general principles. If what he says is taken at face value he would be contradicting Jesus, who clearly says in Matthew that divorce (and remarriage) is permissible in certain circumstances. And to make an obvious point – if a woman is legitimately divorced from her husband she is not his wife any more – and so this verse would not apply – nor would 1 Corinthians 7:39. Divorce severs the marital link just as death does; it is just that the death of the husband serves the point of Paul's illustration here.

The weakness of the traditional views on 1 Corinthians 7

The traditional views, to harmonise their teaching about the gospel statements, have to say that Paul in 1 Corinthians 7 teaches a new additional concession for divorce based on the faith of the marriage partner. The world is to be told that marriage is held in God's eyes differently between believers and unbelievers. Not only does God (understandably) expect a different standard of behaviour – but the underlying rules are different for Christians. It gives the impression that God is not troubled about how unbelievers behave in their relationships – it is just 'Christian' marriages that matter. While there is a Christian church, comprised of believers, a 'Christian' marriage is a marriage adhering to Christian principles, not a marriage of Christians which has a different set of rules to an unbeliever's marriage. To make such a distinction denies marriage as a creation ordinance.

Paul's 'divorce is permissible' rules – a summary:

- Christ's teaching on marriage was for all marriage. There was not a double standard based on the religious beliefs of each partner.

- Paul did not introduce a new set of rules for mixed

marriages.

- Paul applied the existing rules to mixed marriages in case any in Corinth thought that such a marriage **did** have a different set of rules.

- The teaching about husbands is emphasised, because although Jesus was emphatic in the gospels about the rules for men when he allowed the only exception for divorce to be sexual unfaithfulness, he did not specifically mention what happens if you are married to an unbeliever. There is no new exception. Paul teaches that they must not initiate a divorce, despite Ezra's instruction in the past.

- The teaching about wives is emphasised because wives too might have had similar sensibilities. Also wives knew they could divorce their husbands for a failure to provide; a Christian wife might have considered that an unbelieving husband could not provide for her needs. Paul says, as with the husbands, there are no new exceptions! Stay together! If Jesus had ruled that a wife could never divorce her husband as Mark 10:12 at first seems to imply, then Paul would not have to raise the matter here.

- To both the Christian wives and husbands he teaches that far from being 'polluted' by an unbelieving spouse, the situation gives them opportunity to benefit their partner - so stay together.

- A husband, whether a believer or not, should not divorce his wife – Christ will stick with his people. But if a man's wife deserts – he cannot be a 'Christ' to a non-existent wife; he can treat her desertion of him as her divorcing him.

- A wife, whether a believer or not, should not divorce her husband, a Christian is told to cling to the Saviour. But if the husband deserts – he is not being 'like' Christ to his wife – she can divorce him.

- A husband, whether a believer or not, is **not** told here – or anywhere else - that he can leave his wife because of her failure to provide for him, or if she is not 'like' the church.

Paul is saying to both groups, those in mixed marriages and those that are not, the rules are the same. God gives different rules in marriage and divorce to men and women, not to different sub-sets of people. But Paul does consider that Christians might have thought they could exercise their divorce rights against unbelievers. Paul tells them they must not do this. Paul does accept that while the **rules** are the same for believers and unbelievers – unbelievers might **behave** differently. And so he tells the Corinthians that the usual divorce rules come into play if an unbeliever deserts.

The Bible is consistent. Paul does not change the rules, or give any new grounds for divorce. He simply applies the 'status quo' to the position of mixed marriages in case any thought that by simply being in a mixed marriage was in itself grounds for divorce.

Key Points

- **Marriage is a creation ordinance - there are not separate rules for believers, unbelievers, or mixed marriages**

- **Desertion by a partner whatever their profession of faith can be accepted as divorce by the deserted partner**

- **Paul does not give a husband any new grounds to initiate a divorce**

---

8 Remarriage after Divorce

For the sake of simplicity and to maintain the thrust of the argument I have so far assumed that divorce means that either party is subsequently free to remarry. This issue will be addressed now.

The Old Testament position

Exodus 21 is clear – the woman who divorced was 'not bound' – she was free to remarry. Also it is seen in Deuteronomy 24 the woman who was divorced by her husband for sexual immorality was allowed to remarry. It is difficult on any analysis of Deuteronomy 24 not to see that divorcees were allowed to remarry. [118] There is no mention of either party being forbidden remarriage, even for the 'guilty' spouse (or as I would prefer - the unfaithful spouse). The only thing forbidden was remarriage to the first husband. Other parts of the Old Testament are impossible to reconcile if remarriage after divorce was not allowed.

Leviticus 18:16 says:-

Do not have sexual relations with your brother's wife; that would dishonour your brother.

Yet Deuteronomy 25:5 says:-

If brothers are living together and one of them dies without a son, his widow must not marry outside the family. Her husband's brother shall take her and marry her and fulfil the duty of a brother-in-law to her.

The explanation? Leviticus 18:16 must be referring to a living divorced brother. If he was not divorced the relationship would be adulterous and there would be no

---

[118] Instone-Brewer covers the extra-biblical data on this comprehensively in 'Divorce and Remarriage in the Bible' Eerdmans 2002 pages 117ff

point in the command. Leviticus is saying even if a man is divorced from his wife his brother must not marry her - he would be dishonoured seeing his ex-wife with his brother. Also this measure was to protect family integrity. Otherwise a wife living in the close proximity of the extended family could become attracted to her brother-in-law and divorce her husband simply in order to marry his brother. The presumption here is that remarriage after divorce was an accepted fact, because if **all** remarriage after divorce was forbidden there would be no point in this command.

This incidentally is an example of a silent implication that was so obvious at the time Moses wrote it that there was no need to state it. What Leviticus must be saying is:-

Do not have sexual relations with your **divorced** *brother's wife; that would dishonour your brother.*

This is the clear presumption; otherwise the two verses contradict each other. It is clear - but it has not always been obvious; the church has been confused by Leviticus 18:16 – as it has in its teaching on divorce – due to not understanding the correct hidden implication. In the 16th century Katherine of Aragon was the widow of the elder brother of Henry VIII. The latter's marriage to her was only allowed by special dispensation from the Pope because of the contemporary understanding of Leviticus 18:16. Then after many years wrangling by theologians on the continent and in the UK, the marriage was annulled on the same basis. Few it seems considered Deuteronomy 25:5 and the silent implication in Leviticus 18:16. No special dispensation was required for the marriage and there was no biblical basis for the annulment.

The New Testament position

Jesus specifically says in Mark and Luke that remarriage after divorce is considered adultery. But it has already been established that Matthew's exceptive clause – *'except for marital unfaithfulness'* - should be included in all the gospel statements, so the key question now is - what is the significance of the exception clause? Does it apply **both** to the divorce **and** the remarriage? In other words if the divorce is allowed when there has been marital unfaithfulness – is remarriage allowed also? The basis of our approach to this must be Matthew, where there is the fullest account of Jesus' teaching.

Matthew 5 and 19

But I tell you that anyone who divorces his wife, except for marital unfaithfulness, causes her to become an adulteress, and anyone who marries the divorced woman commits adultery. [119]

And similarly...

I tell you that anyone who divorces his wife, except for marital unfaithfulness, and marries another woman commits adultery. [120]

Is Jesus saying that providing you divorce your wife for a legitimate reason – that is marital unfaithfulness – then you can remarry? Or is he saying that you can divorce your wife for marital unfaithfulness, but any remarriage is adultery? One way of resolving this is to move the exceptive clause around in the sentence and see if one or other of the above positions can be reproduced more clearly. If this is attempted it can be seen that it is not possible to arrive at the conclusion that Jesus allows divorce but forbids remarriage. Jesus is talking about divorce and remarriage - one situation, not two. It is difficult to see how Jesus could express himself more clearly than he did. [121]

    A legitimate divorce means that remarriage is possible. In other words the exceptive clause applies to both the divorce and the remarriage. It is the nature of the

---

[119] Matthew 5:32
[120] Matthew 19:9
[121] In my view Thomas Edgar deals with this matter comprehensively and conclusively in 'Divorce and Remarriage' Inter Varsity Press 1990 p156 ff.

divorce that pre-determines the validity of any subsequent marriage.

What about the unfaithful partner?

Much as we might have liked to see Jesus teach on this, he does not. When asked about Deuteronomy 24 Jesus did not comment on whether the woman so described (the unfaithful partner) should have been allowed to remarry or not. This is a surprising omission if it is believed that the Bible forbids remarriage to one party after divorce. Either both parties to the former marriage are divorced, or they are not. If they are so divorced, then both parties are free to remarry. If not then neither party can remarry. [122] It must surely then be assumed that the Old Testament position stands.

The only possible basis for the unfaithful partner not being allowed to remarry is that in some way he or she is no longer suitable for marriage – ever. Or it is being suggested that there is another unforgivable sin, that of breaking the marriage vows. There is no biblical teaching for either of these views.

One argument used is that in Old Testament Israel the death penalty was invoked for the unfaithful partner – so obviously denying them remarriage. But this argument does not stand up to scrutiny, being wrong in its interpretation of the Old Testament position and wrong in its application in the church today – in that it takes an Old Testament punishment (not the principle) and makes a doctrine from it that is binding in the Christian era. (See Appendix 2:The Levitical Death Penalty). In any case if the Old Testament is being appealed to there is the witness of Deuteronomy 24 where the sexually impure partner was allowed to remarry. [123]

If the view is held that only the faithful partner can remarry, then there can be some striking pastoral anomalies

---

[122] See John Murray 'Divorce' Presbyterian and Reformed 1961 p100 ff
[123] Although some argue that the 'something indecent' in that passage is not a sexual matter. See Appendix1: Deuteronomy 24

which will be discussed in Chapter 10. Some churches seek to avoid the potential pitfalls by refusing to marry a couple when either have been divorced from a previous marriage, whether they can be identified as the faithful partner or not. But I know of no church that attempts to vouch for the virginity of a never previously married couple. By implication this position censures adultery but accepts fornication. [124]
Where the commentaries that take this position have gone wrong is seeing the issue as - who was at fault. In contrast the Bible says the issue is – is the marriage over? If the marriage has ended in a divorce based on biblical grounds – the marriage is over – for both parties, and remarriage is legitimate for both.

    The Bible is consistent in its teaching throughout, in that it is the validity of the divorce that determines the status of the subsequent relationship. If the marriage did not end with a divorce based on biblical grounds Jesus teaches the subsequent marriage is 'adultery'. Once this principle is grasped the Bible's teaching comes into clearer focus. This is seen in the Deuteronomy 24 situation. The woman's right to remarry is not questioned – despite her being – in the terms of the traditional view – the 'guilty party'.[125] Why not? Because her original marriage is over. Her status is that of a single woman. As is the case in divorce law in the UK today.

What about the 'remain unmarried' of 1 Corinthians 7?

But it has been seen in the consideration of this passage that every divorce certificate in contemporary Jewish society (and many in the Graeco-Roman world) used similar wording to that used by Paul to indicate that the couple were free to remarry if they wished. [126] It is inconceivable that Paul would use the same words in 1 Corinthians 7, without any qualification, to mean anything but the same thing.

---

[124] And in fact a never married man might have been adulterous if he had had an affair with a married woman.

[125] Of course the unfaithful spouse is guilty of sin, but guilt or innocence is not a concept the Bible uses to decide if a remarriage is valid.

[126] Instone Brewer 'Divorce and Remarriage in the Bible' Eerdmans 2002 p200 ff

What about 1 Timothy 3:2?

Now the overseer must be above reproach, the husband of but one wife...

The argument here is if divorce and remarriage are acceptable then why should an overseer (elder) only have had one wife? The most convincing explanation is that Paul was telling the church that an overseer must only have one wife at a time – unlike many of the Old Testament saints. [127]

The only difficulty with this interpretation is that the teaching about widows in 1 Timothy 5:9 has the same wording. A principle of exegesis would suggest that it should be translated the same way - which would then say a widow should only have had one husband at a time - a very unlikely event. NIV however translates 1 Timothy 5:9 as:-

No widow may be put on the list of widows unless she is over sixty, has been faithful to her husband...

This translation in my view is to be preferred. A further problem, if 'one wife at a time' is not the interpretation, is that Paul's comments and the consequent barring from eldership would apply to a man who was widowed and had remarried. In other words an unmarried divorcee is acceptable but a remarried widower is not. Any other explanation than the one above leads to idealising the 'one wife' concept that is so close to the sacramental view. [128]

What about remarriage after an unbiblical divorce?

It has been seen that in Old Testament Israel a wife could

---

[127] Many commentators say that Paul could not have meant this because polygamy was unknown at the time of writing. However it is now known that the writings found in the 1st century Palestine's Essene community, where they forbade the taking of another wife, were not forbidding remarriage but the taking of a second wife.

[128] Another possible explanation, but less convincing, is that Paul is saying that an overseer must have a wife – that is be married – but this would exclude Paul – and the Lord himself from eldership.

leave her husband if she was not provided for by him – but he had to issue the divorce certificate. Without it no man would take her as a wife as he would effectively be taking the wife of another man. The new husband had to be convinced that no other man had a prior claim on her otherwise he would be guilty of adultery. Although the death penalty was not always extracted for this it was nonetheless a serious sin.

So the position Jesus outlines in the gospels is the same – without a valid divorce the wife cannot take another husband – if she did, he says it is adultery. I do not want to remove the force of Jesus' words. It is a stark reality that a divorce undertaken without there being biblical grounds is a sin in the eyes of the Saviour, and there is therefore an impact on any subsequent relationship. The view that many have taken is that if the divorce is unbiblical – it didn't happen at all – the couple are still married. [129] This certainly makes sense of Jesus' words that remarriage in this situation is adultery.

But should we take this comment by Jesus to mean literally, that any couple so divorced who go on to marry other partners, are in an ongoing state of adultery? I believe that there should be some caution about taking such a view for four reasons:-

> **1.** In what sense can a couple still be married if they have separated and are pursuing another life, often with a different partner, even having children by them? We must go back again to the definition of marriage. If the state is allowed to define marriage, any couple who are still legally married, are certainly married for tax and property purposes, no matter what their personal circumstances.
>
> But even the state recognises that a separated husband does not necessarily have sexual rights over his wife. And we should be clear - the modern secular state and the mind of God are two different

---

[129] Until recently the Church of England considered all remarriage after divorce adultery.

things. If in God's word a marriage is a covenant relationship between a man and woman to serve the five fold purpose outlined in Chapter 1 - how can such a separated couple, cohabiting with new, different partners, be still 'married' to their original partners?

Also it has been seen in Chapter 7 that there is no concept in the New Testament era of a long term separated but still married state. [130] This view, that a couple who have had an unbiblical divorce are still married in the eyes of God, can only apply if you have a sacramental view of marriage, that marriage is an unalterable act done by God in heaven.

2. Jesus uses the word adultery in the aorist tense – implying that the initial act in the new relationship is adulterous, but the ongoing relationship should not necessarily be viewed as sinful. [131]

3. Jesus is quite capable of using the term adultery in a non-literal, non-legal way – for example in Matthew 5:28:-

But I tell you that anyone who looks at a [married] woman lustfully has already committed adultery with her in his heart.

Should such a man be disciplined by his church, or forbidden marriage?

4. God blessed the great King David's subsequent relationship with Bathsheba even though it began in a clearly adulterous manner. Nathan criticized David for his sin; there was much regret, pain, tears, and repentance; but Nathan is not recorded as saying

---

[130] Instone-Brewer 'Divorce and Remarriage in the Bible' Eerdmans 2002 p190. See also Stephen Clark 'Putting Asunder...' Bryntirion Press 1999 pp 137-143 for the contemporary social background to Paul's letter.

[131] See Laney 'Divorce and Remarriage' Inter Varsity Press 1990 p39

that David had to give Bathsheba up, or that he was no longer fit to be a prophet. [132]

Certain sins are facts. If you steal an apple, no matter that the Bible forbids it - it is stolen. If it is eaten, or gone rotten, exact restitution is not possible. Some things cannot be undone. Some couples have undoubtedly divorced without valid grounds and remarried. It is a sin.

But it is not the unforgivable sin; Jesus' use of the aorist tense and the specific example of the repentant David and Bathsheba implies we should not consider the subsequent relationship an ongoing adultery. Surely any sin truly repented of should be forgiven, and in the case of an unbiblical divorce the subsequent relationship considered valid.

Marriage in disrepute?

I am sympathetic with the view that is sincerely held by some that this freedom of the unfaithful partner to remarry, and the acceptance of remarried couples who have had an unbiblical divorce, could bring marriage into disrepute. People could freely enter into one marriage after another, breaking their vows in each. The practical consequences of this teaching will be considered in Chapter 10.

A conclusion

Without a prior assumption that remarriage is forbidden after divorce, it is difficult to see how any analysis of the teachings in the Bible could come to such a view. And although to forbid remarriage to the unfaithful partner does in some ways appear logical, it is not taught in the Bible – and goes against the principle of forgiveness for any repentant sinner seen elsewhere in the New Testament.

Jesus condemns an unbiblical divorce saying that any subsequent marriage relationship is tantamount to adultery, but his careful choice of the verb's tense and the Bible's

---

[132] 2 Samuel 12

teaching as a whole shows that there is grace even in this situation.

> **Key Points**
>
> - **When a couple divorce both parties are divorced and both parties are free to remarry. Their freedom to remarry is predicated on the validity of their divorce, not the supposed 'guilt' or 'innocence' of either partner.**
>
> - **A couple divorced without biblical grounds are considered to be still married and any subsequent marriage consequently 'adulterous'**
>
> - **Such adultery should not be considered as a legal definition and God's forgiveness is available for such a remarried couple**

9 Various Objections Considered

This thesis:-

- **makes divorce too easy**

This thesis does allow a woman to initiate a divorce for reasons other than, but including, the sexual unfaithfulness of her husband. She is not forced, based on the clear teaching of Exodus 21, to stay with a husband against her will. Neither marriage, nor divorce, should be entered into lightly. I believe the local church should play a much more active part in advising couples just what the marital obligations are and only conduct a marriage ceremony when those obligations are fully understood and witnessed by the local congregation. Counselling should also occur before a divorce and everything possible done to keep the marriage together in a God honouring way.

- **sets the cause of women's equality back**

It is true that women in the Bible do have different and more generous grounds for divorce than men. But that is God's way. It is also God's way that women generally are reluctant to end a marriage even when it is less than ideal. The different grounds for divorce serve two purposes – to reflect Christ and the church – and to protect women.

- **means that men can be sexually unfaithful with impunity**

No. It is true that a man in Old Testament Israel could have more than one wife – but even then this did not stop a wife divorcing a husband for taking a second wife – indeed this is in effect the Exodus 21 teaching.

- **leaves men without the option for divorce from difficult or abusive wives**

But this thesis shares this position with the traditional views

- this is a necessary out working of the picture of Christ and the church. There is no easy answer to this problem. A husband in such a situation would need much grace and support from his church.

- **is teaching a doctrine based on the Lord's silence**

However it is not the Bible's silence. Jesus did not specifically mention Exodus 21, but as has been seen the theme of that chapter is picked up in Ephesians 5 and 1 Corinthians 7. What the traditional views are saying by default is that Jesus **removes** the woman's grounds for divorce outlined in Exodus 21 by his silence on the subject. Silence usually means the status quo is retained. The weight of evidence lies therefore with this thesis.

- **is teaching that an obscure verse in Exodus applies today**

The Exodus teaching that a wife can expect to be provided for by her husband is the repeated example in the Old Testament era. The husband was head of the household and it was a presumption that he had ultimate responsibility to provide for that household. It was the basis of virtually all Jewish marriages in the Old Testament. The teaching is repeated in the New Testament, specifically in Ephesians 5 and generally in the teaching about the nature of a husband's role. Virtually all divorces initiated by women in Old Testament Israel were based on the provision of Exodus 21.[133] Paul uses the same argument and very similar language in 1 Corinthians 7. The grounds for divorce in Exodus were the basis of the teaching of both the Hillelites and Shammaites in first century Palestine. It would be odd if when supporting the Shammaites' interpretation of Deuteronomy 24 Jesus did not correct their other views on divorce. If he did the Bible does not record it.

---

[133] See Instone-Brewer 'Divorce and Remarriage in the Bible' Eerdmans 2002 Chapter 2 & p117ff

- **is teaching that the church has been wrong all these years**

The Roman Catholic teaching that marriage is a sacrament was the predominant position in Europe for more than a thousand years. In the 16th century Erasmus came up with the view widely held in the evangelical community today. He did not have access to the scholarship we have today which has enabled us to see the context of the New Testament teaching more clearly. As pointed out in Chapter 4 Christians throughout church history have often had an ambivalent attitude to human sexuality; any teaching that seemed more 'strict' was seen as more likely to be the true teaching of the Bible, and subsequently embraced as a doctrine in the church.

The various combinations of the traditional views:-

- **teach that there is a radical discontinuity between the Testaments**

A discontinuity that is not seen in any other area.

- **rely for their teaching on something the Bible does not say**

That the wife's **only** ground for divorce is her husband's sexual unfaithfulness.

- **look to find an 'innocent party'**

Those that hold this view are in the invidious position of deciding who is the innocent partner, as if there is such a thing in any marriage. To assume the faithful partner is guiltless shows a lack of sensitivity to life's realities.

- **give the impression there is another unforgivable sin**

That of being a 'guilty' partner in marriage.

- **create a double standard**

Nowhere does the Bible say a husband must divorce his wife for her sexual unfaithfulness. Any church leadership should, or at least could, presuppose that the first line of counselling is that the husband might forgive his wife - as God did with Israel so many times. However if a divorce does take place, in forbidding remarriage to the wife, the church appears to be saying they will not forgive her - although it was suggested that the wronged husband might do so.

- **turn a blind eye to fornication yet penalise those that marry**

When a couple who are both single come forward for marriage their previous private lives are not usually subject to investigation, but often a once married man or woman is prohibited from marrying.

- **can tempt a couple into sin**

A not uncommon situation is for a marriage to have irretrievably broken down, but there has been no infidelity. The couple is advised that there is no possibility of divorce, unless there has been infidelity. So this route can then become the easy way out of the marriage, especially if the church does offer forgiveness for a sinner, even for those involved in sexual sins.

- **are often pastorally 'unworkable'**

The husband is an alcoholic, a wife beater - even a murderer, but because he has not committed a sexual sin the wife would be told in some (many?) churches that she cannot divorce him. If instead she murdered her husband and was eventually released from prison, she would be more readily accepted in some churches than if she **had** divorced him.

- **give the impression that there are different rules for unbelievers**

By teaching that the divorce rules are different in a 'mixed' marriage, the impression is given that God is less interested in the sexual morality of unbelievers.

- **bind a believer by the profession of another**

A wife deserted by a 'believing' husband is told that she cannot remarry. Who is to know whether his profession is authentic? What if he is found to be apostate many years later? The deserted wife will have had a life of singleness, bound by the false profession of her deserting husband.

- **lose the picture of Christ and the church**

Perhaps this is the biggest drawback to all the traditional views. By giving the husband and wife the same grounds for divorce, the picture of redemption embedded in marriage and divorce is lost.

10 A Practical Outworking

Getting married

Perhaps there would be less marital breakdown if before a couple married more time was spent in counselling about the roles the Bible expects to see in that relationship. Too often couples contemplating marriage are asked to 'seek the Lord's will' - often meaning that an attempt is to be made to interpret providential signposts; to 'pray about it' – not a bad thing – but to what end? All these things are an inadequate preparation for taking on a lifetime commitment.

The man should have the role of the husband explained to him and the woman the role of a wife. Not as to specifics – but with the great biblical theme of Christ and the church uppermost in the counsellor's mind. Indeed it might be said that if the prospective husband does not have the same reaction to his counsellor that the disciples had to Jesus when he taught about marriage - the counsellor has not done his job.

The comment made by the disciples? :-

...if this is the situation between a husband and wife, it is better not to marry. [134]

A biblically valid divorce

I will attempt here to show which scenarios can give rise to a biblically valid divorce. If the couple have registered the marriage with the state then there will be legal and financial issues to handle which often involve a solicitor – even if both parties are Christians and it is an 'amicable'

---

[134] Matthew 19:10

divorce. [135] Any comment or advice about this is obviously beyond the scope of this book. In all the situations I give as examples the presumption must be that every effort should be made to maintain the marriage and keep the couple together if that can be done at all in a God honouring way.

In these scenarios I am not looking to allocate blame or identify who the sinful partner is. It is up to the spiritual oversight of a church to decide what action to take in a case of any perceived sinful behaviour by a church member, whether it be in a marriage relationship or not. Such action might be to do nothing at all, to exercise some form of church discipline, or to the extreme position of excommunication from the fellowship. [Matthew 18:15-18]

John and Susan

John and Susan are Christians but are having difficulties, there are many arguments, mostly over money. In both their minds they have come to the end, and want a divorce. There has been no infidelity.

John cannot initiate a divorce; Susan must decide if John is providing for her adequately. If he is, Susan should be counselled to accept John's headship and a real attempt made to find some way through the problem they have. If

---

[135] The legal status of marriage in the UK and the law's ruling on the division of assets can often inject a note of acrimony into any divorce that makes dispassionate counselling difficult. A further complication is provision for the children. As we have seen in Old Testament Israel divorce was a private matter. The husband had to provide for his wife for the rest of her life (and it seems for the children to adulthood). If the wife initiated a divorce she could take from the marriage what she brought into it but no more, and the husband's responsibilities to her then ceased. If she was guilty of sexual immorality she left the marriage with nothing. The equal division of assets widely accepted in the West today, while seemingly fair, has led inadvertently to the decline in the number of couples marrying. The increasing personal financial wealth of both men and women, and later, and second, or even third marriages, means many are reluctant to accept this status quo, and for this reason many in the older generation to my personal knowledge do not want their children to register their relationship with the state.

John is not providing for her and is unable or unwilling to do so – then ultimately Susan can initiate a divorce. Even then the pastoral advice must be to emphasise that John never really could be Jesus Christ to her, that we are all fallen creatures, and every effort should be made to get the marriage back on track. But in the end if Susan wants to go – she can. [Exodus 21:10-11]

Bill and Mary

Bill is a Christian but Mary isn't. There are difficulties. Mary leaves.

Bill is not bound, he can divorce. [1 Corinthians 7:15]

Darren and Jennifer

- are both Christians but Jennifer deserts Darren. No other person is involved.

Darren is free, Jennifer has effectively divorced him. [Exodus 21:10,11]

Ken and Lynda

Are both Christians but Ken has an affair.

Lynda can choose to forgive Ken and this should be the first option. However she can initiate a divorce for the sexual unfaithfulness - on the basis that Ken has been 'unreasonable' and not treated her as Christ would. If Ken's unfaithful relationship was with a married woman he has been guilty of adultery against that other marriage, if with a single woman he is guilty of sexual immorality.
[Exodus 21:10,11]

Bob and Ruth

Are both believers. Ruth has an affair.

Bob is free, but not compelled, to divorce her. [Matthew

5:32; 19:9]

Barry and Helen

Both are believers but Helen simply walks out on Barry for another man.

Barry can have a biblical divorce because his wife has opted to leave him – even if in the minds of some her reason for leaving was not valid – because Helen has initiated a divorce by leaving him. Helen has in any case been sexually unfaithful.
[Exodus 21:10,11 Matthew 5:32   19:9]

Christine and David

Are both believers. Christine simply decides 'she does not love David anymore' and leaves him.

Christine has separated and so David is entitled to assume that she is divorcing him. It becomes a valid divorce – even though Christine's action appears to have been unwarranted.
[Exodus 21:10,11]

Geoff and Carol

Carol is an abusive and difficult wife. Geoff wants out of the relationship and divorces Carol.

Geoff should not have initiated a divorce. This divorce is unbiblical.
[Matthew 5:32   19:9]

Christ and the church

A biblical divorce means that the divorce is within the permitted circumstances outlined in the Bible. As has been seen the validity of the divorce is the touchstone of the nature of any subsequent relationship. A valid divorce means that both parties can remarry.

A biblically valid divorce does not mean that there was no sin or that either party is guiltless. A person who has had a valid divorce might be the unfaithful partner, so obviously they are not without sin. Indeed as outlined in the introduction all divorce is the outcome of sin. A divorce that was not valid biblically means that the original marriage in principle still stands in Christ's eyes.

If these hypothetical circumstances are reviewed it can be seen that there is only one divorce that is 'unbiblical' – where a husband leaves his wife when she has been sexually faithful. Why is this divorce unbiblical? Because the Bible never gives the husband the right to divorce in this situation. Why is this? It is that all important picture of Christ and the church. The individual believer can walk away from Christ. But Christ will never walk away from his elect. Anything that suggests this within the marriage/divorce picture is not permitted by God. But Christ will disown those that disown him, [136] so a husband can divorce his wife if she goes with another man, but otherwise Christ will deliver the church intact to God at the end of the age.

In contrast any divorce where a wife has left her husband is in effect a biblical (not sinless) divorce. It might be thought by the leadership of the church that she had no good reason to leave – but how do they know? Marriage is a public matter but the marriage relationship itself is a very private thing. Exodus 21 and 1 Corinthians 7 allows the wife to leave her husband for his unreasonable behaviour. And the theology? Christ does not hold believers to himself against their will.

Remarriage - for those who have had a biblical divorce

When it comes to remarriage the basis of a previous divorce will have to be considered even if it is known to be a biblically valid divorce. While a valid divorce means that the couple are as single people before God, it does not mean that there was no sin. The basis of any consideration is not to

---

[136] 2 Timothy 2:11-13

forbid or permit remarriage, but to inform the advice given to the couple. A single man, whether previously married or not, might present himself to be married, but known to the church leadership he has a history of abusive relationships with women. They might choose not to conduct a marriage service for him in that it might bring their fellowship into disrepute - but they could not forbid him marriage, or if he married elsewhere say that his marriage was in some way invalid.

A couple might have had a biblically valid divorce in that the husband initiated a divorce for his wife's unfaithfulness, but the person presenting for remarriage is the unfaithful wife. Here again wisdom by the oversight of the church and knowledge of the person is required. Presumably the church leadership will look to see if repentance is evidenced and there is a full understanding of the obligations of the new marriage, and the new husband is aware of the past. If the sexual unfaithfulness had occurred within the fellowship it might be wisest to counsel the couple to join another fellowship and seek to have the marriage there.

Every situation has to be treated individually. This applies to all marriage and especially remarriage after divorce. Prior knowledge of the parties will inform the counselling, because even when a 'faithful' divorced partner presents for marriage, or a divorced woman who feels she was not provided for in her previous marriage, guiltlessness cannot be assumed. But there is nothing per se to forbid the remarriage.

It might be decided to have a short service of repentance – in public or private - before any new marriage ceremony; it is entirely up to the pastoral oversight of the fellowship and the couple involved. But to deny remarriage to either party after a biblically valid divorce is unscriptural.

Remarriage - for those who have had an unbiblical divorce

This is effectively where a husband has left his wife even though she has been sexually faithful – for example Geoff and Carol. If Carol is still alone, and she wants Geoff back, and he is not prepared to go back to her – then the church is, on biblical grounds, entitled to deny him marriage to a new partner. If Carol has married somebody else, or she does not want Geoff back – she has effectively divorced him, and the situation is now different. Geoff is theoretically free to remarry. But it might be that the church feels Geoff has acted as an unbeliever and should be treated as such whether Carol would have him back or not. [137] It could be for practical reasons in this case that the oversight of the church are not prepared to conduct a new marriage even though Geoff and his intended wife are eligible biblically.

It is open then to the church leaders to point out that although the new marriage is permissible, for practical reasons the couple ought to seek a new fellowship to join and marry there. But to forbid somebody marriage simply because of some past sin is not only not scriptural but actually goes against the teaching of the apostle Paul. [138]

A conclusion

While the theology of remarriage after divorce is clear, the decisions to be made about any such remarriage of a couple within any particular fellowship might not be. Some might consider it hypocritical to suggest that in some cases within a local fellowship it might be wisest to ask a couple to marry elsewhere, on the basis that although the remarriage is legitimate, the church oversight was not happy about conducting the service. But what is legitimate is not always wise. Sometimes even though you would not personally commission an act, even though legitimate, you might accept it once it is done.

Consider again David and Bathsheba. David married Bathsheba after his adultery with her, and after he had ensured that Uriah had been killed in battle. (2 Samuel 11:26,27). *But the thing David had done displeased the Lord.* What displeased the Lord was David's adultery and murder. God condemned David for that. No comment is made about his subsequent marriage to Bathsheba. Would Nathan, the

---

[137] Matthew 18:15-18
[138] 1 Timothy 4:1-3

A Practical Outworking

prophet who condemned David, have conducted a marriage service for Bathsheba and David? I think this is highly unlikely. The Jewish (not biblical) perspective was that a man could not marry a woman he had been adulterous with (see footnote 79). But once presented with the marriage Nathan accepted the status quo. There was nothing in Old Testament teaching to forbid it. Nathan took the subsequent message from God that their second child (their firstborn child died) be named Jedidiah - 'loved of God' (2 Samuel 12:24,25); God blessed this marriage with the birth of Solomon, who figures in the genealogy of Christ.

11 The Key Points

Introduction

- Five 'rules' of exegesis will be used

- Marriage is an earthly picture of a believer's redemption in Christ and this can further help us to understand the biblical basis for divorce

1   Marriage – a Covenant

- Marriage is a picture of the relationship between Christ and the church

- Marriage is a covenant relationship with gender based roles

- Marriage is a heterosexual couple choosing to go through life together with a covenant of permanence (even if only implied), consummated with sexual intercourse

2   Marriage – a One Flesh Union

- The 'one flesh' union of marriage means that the couple form a new family unit

- Marriage is not a sacrament and not a mystical union

- The sexual act without a 'covenant' is not marriage

- Marriage is a protected symbol of Christ and the church

3   Traditional Views

- Probably the most widely held view about divorce in the evangelical community is:- Divorce for sexual unfaithfulness or desertion, and remarriage for the

The Key Points

'innocent' party

4   The Thesis

- Exodus 21 outlines the rules for a woman initiating a divorce against her husband

- Deuteronomy 24 outlines the rules for a man initiating a divorce against his wife

- Jesus emphasises principles and answers the specific question he was asked

- 1 Corinthians 7 permits either a husband or wife to treat their partner's desertion as a divorce

5   The Old Testament and Divorce

- Divorce was allowed by God after the Fall of man and is not in itself sinful

- The Old Testament rules governing divorce are gender specific

- Divorce for the man is allowed if his wife is sexually impure

- Divorce for the woman is allowed if in her own opinion her husband is not faithful to his task

6   Jesus and Divorce

- The teaching of the Old Testament and the New Testament is consistent

- Jesus' general statements about divorce are just that – statements of general principle

- Jesus did not cancel the Old Testament concessions on divorce – he clarified those he was asked about

7 Paul and Divorce

- Marriage is a creation ordinance - there are not separate rules for believers, unbelievers, or mixed marriages

- Desertion by a partner whatever their profession of faith can be accepted as divorce by the deserted partner

- Paul does not give a husband any new grounds to initiate a divorce

8 Remarriage after Divorce

- When a couple divorce both parties are divorced and both parties are free to remarry. Their freedom to remarry is predicated on the validity of their divorce, not the supposed 'guilt' or 'innocence' of either partner.

- A couple divorced without biblical grounds are considered to be still married and any subsequent marriage consequently 'adulterous'

- Such adultery should not be considered as a legal definition and God's forgiveness is available for such a remarried couple

12 A Conclusion

Adam and Eve walked in that garden in paradise and knew the presence of God. Since then God has spoken directly only to his appointed prophets and apostles. Only Moses was allowed up the mountain and spoke with God in the burning bush, although several thousands will have seen the Tabernacle, witnessed the brass serpent on the pole, and God's miraculous provision of food and water in Israel's desert wanderings. But only a few saw Christ as he walked this earth, and only three of the disciples heard the heavenly voice on the Mount of Transfiguration.

In contrast every man, woman, and child in the world has been brought to existence through heterosexual intercourse.[139] And it was God's intention that this should only be within the context of marriage - indeed its absence defines its immorality. So it was God's purpose that every member of the human race will have seen in marriage an enduring and powerful picture of the church's relationship to Christ. This surely is the supreme purpose of marriage.

And divorce? It was allowed because of sin, the grounds for divorce being based on the redemption picture. In other words when the covenantal picture is broken by men and women's sinfulness, divorce is reluctantly allowed by a compassionate God. Surely any exegesis of divorce in the New Testament has to take into account this fact, as well as the specific teaching of Scripture elsewhere.

The essence of the problem has been what Jesus meant in Mark 10:12:-

... And if she divorces her husband and marries another man, she commits adultery

These thirteen words, in which Jesus forbids divorce to wives, cannot be the whole story for every situation. This is widely

---

[139] Excluding Adam and Eve, and Christ himself; and recent technological advances that have enabled various other forms of conception

accepted in the evangelical community. But instead of giving wives their own exception clause so widely understood at the time – the traditional views give to them the exception clause that belonged to the husband. The church then has built on this shaky foundation a teaching that loses the redemption picture, and when examined, is seen to be a fragile edifice that does not stand up to scrutiny.

I think it is clear that there are only two possibilities:-

1. The statement by Christ in Mark 10:12 stands as it is written and is binding – so Jesus removes all the Old Testament teaching about wives and divorce. (The Roman Catholic Church embraces this view.)

2. All the Old Testament teaching stands and this statement complements it by repeating the general principle. (This thesis.)

What I do not believe is possible to argue on any reasonable exegetical grounds is that there is a third scenario. A scenario that says:-

- Mark 10:12 revokes all the Old Testament position for wives and teaches a new doctrine.
- The new doctrine, a new exception clause for wives, is not stated anywhere in the Bible – so it has to be imported from the secular world's ideas of gender equality - and then Jesus' audience is to be imagined as assuming it is there.
- To this is added the 'Pauline exception' – where it is considered that Paul says there are different rules in mixed marriages. This teaching is deduced from 1 Corinthians 7 where the whole thrust of Paul's argument is that the same rules apply.

This is the position the traditional views rely on. Backed up by the flawed and false application of a little understood lapsed Levitical punishment that was for a specific sexual sin – adultery - not for the broader 'sexual unfaithfulness' that the traditional views teach.

Why have we gone so wrong?

- The true covenantal purpose of marriage has been obscured by Western secular Romanticism. The personal, emotional, and sexual dimensions of the relationship have become the all important aspect of marriage.

- Equality has been confused with sameness.

- Sexual sins have become the *bête noire* of the Christian community - and seen as the defining sin for divorce purposes. In other words sexual sins, and those alone, become grounds for divorce in their own right, not because of any break in the covenantal picture.

It is true a husband is only allowed to divorce for his wife's sexual sins – but why? Is it because, as many seem to think, this was the worst sin a wife might commit? No. Jesus said that to reject the Son of God was worse than any sin committed at Sodom; [140] yet Paul specifically says that a husband is not to divorce his wife even if she has rejected the Saviour.

Divorce for sexual sin by the wife is specifically allowed because it breaks the covenantal picture. Biblical divorce rules were never based on the gravity of any particular sin, but on the impact they had on the redemptive picture.

This thesis has relied on what the text of the Bible says. However using the model of Christ and the church it can be seen why the Bible teaches these specific gender-based grounds for divorce. The basis of divorce in the Bible is not sexual sins per se, bad though they are; the basis for divorce is a broken picture of Christ and his church.

Divorce has for many years in the church been the unmentionable, if not the unforgivable, sin. Divorce is the product of sin, given to man because of sin, yet not itself

---
[140] Matthew 11:23,24

sin. A hospital, also a product of the Fall, is no more sinful than divorce. And a hospital?

- No one wants to be there
- People there are innocent victims – and culprits of self-harm or carelessness
- We should have compassion on them all

- and so we should have compassion for all those that have suffered a divorce.

To some this thesis might seem radical and liberal. Radical in its use of the Old Testament, and the redemptive picture of Christ and the church, as a guide to the New Testament's teaching on divorce. Radical in its rejection of centuries of traditional divorce teaching offered by the church. Liberal in that it seems to be generous in allowing a wife to initiate a divorce for the failure of her husband to provide for her on her own terms; that she alone defines what is 'unreasonable' – no pastor, no judge, to decide for her. But a review of many of the divorce books published for the evangelical community shows that the authors, many of them experienced pastors, would allow a wife to initiate a divorce for reasons other than a husband's sexual sins.

Several rely on the fact that the church is able in certain circumstances (based on Matthew 18) to view a difficult husband as if he was an unbeliever. They then invoke the teaching of 1 Corinthians 7 where Paul teaches that you may divorce (an unbeliever) for desertion. Some interpreting neglect as desertion even though the spouse is still very much there. [141] This might in certain circumstances be a valid route. But I believe this thesis embraces a more consistent exegesis of the texts and a more coherent theological position.

Even on a practical level, if the husband is head of the household, and the wife is not allowed a divorce except for his marital unfaithfulness – it is a potential recipe for tyranny. Obviously this is not God's intention, but we are in

---

[141] For example Stephen Clark 'Putting Asunder' Bryntyrion Press 1999 p188

a fallen world; that is why he allowed divorce for a husband's unreasonable behaviour.

From the husband's perspective – he is head of the household – so how the marriage works is very much down to him. What would be the basis of him initiating a separation apart from his wife's infidelity? The head of a university department does not leave because he has a difficult lecturer to cope with. It is the other way round! The husband is head of the household and does not leave the household because of a difficult wife. But the wife can leave if she does not feel fairly treated by her husband. The teaching of the Bible is ever practical, ever wise.

All about Christ and the church

It is understandable that murder is wrong, that it is wrong to bear false witness, and wrong to steal; they are all sins that clearly damage other people. Also it is wrong to worship another God – our God is a jealous God and our praise should be for him alone.

Adultery similarly damages others - but how can any other consensual sexual act between two adults be immoral? Why is homosexual sex always wrong? What makes even heterosexual sex, outside marriage, immoral? It is all Christ and the church. This is the supreme purpose of the marriage act – it consummates the one family union that reflects the union of a believer with his Lord – and is in itself a glimpse of the pleasure of the consummation of the ages when Christ comes for his church. For these reasons it should only be enjoyed in a relationship that reflects that great theme. So the relationship must be:

- heterosexual: Christ is a man and his people are always portrayed as a female bride
- covenantal : because Christ has a covenant with his people
- consensual: because no one is forced to come to Christ

Once these ingredients are in place – the sexual act is not a sin. It is the absence of these ingredients that defines its immorality. [142] So without any detailed knowledge of the Bible – the morality of every sexual act can be determined from the relationship of Christ to the church.

And so it is with divorce. A Christian need not concern himself with the detailed exegesis that has been considered in this thesis – but instead go again to the relationship of Christ and his church. Is it permitted for a wife to leave her husband? Can a husband divorce his wife? What if a wife deserts? All the answers are there. It is all Christ and the church.

To display to the world – Christ and the church

God designed the world, and marriage, for us. Even divorce was for our benefit – albeit a concession. But the great theme in marriage and divorce is not these practical issues, rather the theology of redemption. God wants marriages to display to the world this great redemptive theme. Genesis, Exodus, Deuteronomy, Mathew, Mark, Luke and 1 Corinthians all follow the same path; marriage is a life long creation ordinance with gender specific roles to picture the relationship of Christ and the church. Grounds for divorce follow directly from that teaching. This thesis I believe allows all the Bible verses that refer to divorce to breathe this message, without the twists and turns and dissonance that the traditional views demand, and sometimes allude to, in their own expositions.

As has been seen, symbols are important to God. The church should not allow the picture of the believer's relationship to Christ, and Christ's ongoing ministry to his church, portrayed so wondrously in marriage, to be compromised by taking into its teaching on divorce a secular view of equality and fairness; rather it should share with the world in its biblical perspectives on marriage, and divorce, the glorious themes of redemption and grace.

---

[142] The only exception is incest. But interestingly marriage with close relatives must have occurred in the early years of the human race. It is now known that the degradation of the gene pool means that when close relations produce offspring there is a risk of genetic mutation. So the subsequent Levitical prohibition is one to protect persons – not necessarily preventing intrinsic immorality.

Appendix 1: Deuteronomy 24

Some of those that hold the traditional views believe that Hillel and his followers were correct in their interpretation of Deuteronomy, that the Hebrew word ' *'erwat'* - *'something indecent'* - in Deuteronomy 24 cannot be sexual impurity, but instead some arbitrary thing that displeased a husband.

This interpretation of Jesus' reply to the Pharisees goes like this:-

- The Deuteronomy passage is not about the sexual unfaithfulness of the wife, because for that there would be the death penalty.
- Moses allowed a temporary concession for some arbitrary thing that displeased the husband.
- The 'hard hearts' that Jesus refers to in Matthew 19 belong to the Old Covenant Jews, for which there is no place under the New Covenant, where God has sent the *'Spirit of his Son into our hearts'*. (Galatians 4:6)
- Jesus removed this concession of Moses and replaced it with divorce for sexual unfaithfulness only.

Thirteen reasons why this interpretation is flawed:

1   The death penalty was for adultery only, not for other sexual sins and in any case was not always enforced.

2   The word ' *'erwat* ' is used in Leviticus 18 to refer to the nakedness involved in the forbidden sexual relationships listed there, and similarly in Ezekiel 16 where the word is used to refer to the shame of nakedness.

3   ' *'erwat'* is thought by many scholars to refer to some sexual sin, as is evidenced by the translation *'something indecent'* in NIV and *'uncleanness'* in King James Version – both suggesting a sexual matter – not some arbitrary thing that displeased a husband.

4   If Moses did allow divorce for arbitrary reasons it means that a divorce for a trivial reason was according to God's revealed will. A wife could be discarded lightly. Yet Moses taught for a man to take another man's wife was adultery - for which there was the death penalty. Even gathering wood on the Sabbath day would invoke the death penalty (Numbers 15:32-36). Those who hold this traditional view are in effect saying that to discard a wife was acceptable in the Old Testament economy – a 'concession to hard hearts'. But why was there no concession for the wood gatherer?

5   And those 'hard hearts'? When Galatians 4:6 tells us that God has sent the '*Spirit of his Son into our hearts*' it refers to Christians. We must assume that non-Christians retain their hard hearts. Does the Mosaic divorce legislation then still apply to them? Are unbelieving husbands today allowed to divorce their wives for trivial reasons? The hard hearts referred to by Christ surely refer to all humanity tainted by sin since Adam's first act of disobedience in the Garden of Eden.

6   When Jesus addressed the issue of the interpretation of Deuteronomy 24 he was not speaking to Christians or about a 'Christian' marriage – or even about a 'Jewish' marriage. He went right back to Genesis reaffirming that marriage is a creation ordinance. There are not different rules for believers and unbelievers.

7   Why does Jesus teach that divorce is permissible for '*porneia*' – defined by many as sexual impurity, which mirrors the very word that is in dispute in Deuteronomy - if he was **not** confirming that teaching? [143]

---

[143] *Porneia* can refer to the incestuous relationships in Leviticus 18 – and certainly that seems to be its use on Acts 6:20. However the context here is Deuteronomy. Many commentators argue for non-specific sexual immorality as the definition, see particularly Edgar 'Divorce and Remarriage' Inter Varsity Press 1990 p162. NIV appears to have taken this line.

Appendix 1: Deuteronomy

8   Why would Jesus begin his reply to the Pharisees with the phrase *'Haven't you read'* implying, as he does elsewhere in the gospels, that what he is going to say is found in the Old Testament?

9   When Jesus uses the expression *'But I tell you'* in the Sermon on the Mount he does not revoke Old Testament teaching. So we should not expect him to do so when he uses the same expression in his divorce teaching.

10   And, significantly, Jesus in his reply uses the actual wording that the Shammaites used in their teaching.[144] This is an unusual thing to do if he wasn't making it clear that the Shammaites' interpretation of Deuteronomy 24 was the correct one.

11   In effect this traditional interpretation puts the Shammaites in the position of wrongly interpreting Deuteronomy 24 – but in their mistake they had correctly anticipated a new revelation – a new stricter divorce rule!

12   Marriage is a picture of our relationship with God; on what grounds would **he** sever that relationship? God would divorce his 'wife' for 'sexual impurity' (ie idolatry). For the picture to hold, it would be expected that he would allow men to divorce their wives only for sexual impurity. It would run counter to this to assume that Moses allowed divorce for some arbitrary reason.

13   This view of Deuteronomy means that Jesus changed a significant Old Testament teaching. He revoked the Old Testament on a doctrinal point. His teaching is sometimes a repetition of Scripture, sometimes a fulfilment, or even a 'spiritualization' of truths

---

[144] See Instone-Brewer 'Divorce and Remarriage in the Bible' p102 and Cornes 'Divorce and Remarriage' Eerdmans 1993 p201

found there – but never a reversal or dramatic new departure? Can the reader think of any other area where this happens in the New Testament?

Appendix 2: The Levitical Death Penalty

Is there not significance in that there was the death penalty for adultery in the Old Testament?

The traditional views rely heavily on this argument to support their thesis that now a wife has the same (restricted) right of divorce as her husband.

The argument goes like this:

In the Old Testament a wife was released from marriage when her husband was sexually unfaithful because her husband was put to death for the offence. [145] He had broken the 'marriage intimacy'; the Old Testament marriage was effectively dissolved, the wife was free to re-marry; the guilty party, the husband, was dead so he obviously could not.

It is seen as 'only reasonable' to update this teaching into the Christian era and give the wife a right to divorce and remarry on the grounds of her husband's sexual unfaithfulness. The guilty party, the husband, while not being put to death is rather told he can never re-marry. At first this looks persuasive. But the interpretation of Scripture is wrong; its application is wrong; and the principle is wrong.

The interpretation of Scripture

The interpretation of Scripture is wrong because adultery is when a man (whether married or not) takes another man's wife. (See Appendix 4). The man and his lover were put to death for adultery not because it was primarily an offence against either marriage – but against God and his picture of Christ and the church. [146] For other sexual sins there was not the death penalty. If a husband slept with a virgin whom he did not take as a wife, this was sexual immorality,

---

[145] Leviticus 20:10 Deuteronomy 22:22
[146] See comments in Chapter 2 and Appendix 4: Adultery

Divorce and the Bible

penalties were imposed, but not the death penalty. [147] (Of course his wife could divorce him for this lack of sexual faithfulness based on Exodus 21.)

So if those who hold the traditional views that use this argument were being faithful to Scripture, a wife's right to divorce should be restricted to a husband's adultery, not his sexual unfaithfulness [148] – and indeed she should be compelled (not permitted) to divorce him.

The application

The application is wrong because this traditional teaching is based not on the commandment – 'you shall not commit adultery' – but on the discipline for the offence given at a particular time in Israel's history. Christians differ on the application of the Old Testament commandments today. Paul in Galatians says:-

For through the law I died to the law so that I might live for God.[149]

Some take this to mean we are dead to all the Old Testament law – others say that the 'moral' laws, summarised in the Ten Commandments, are still binding. I know of no church grouping that takes the view that the Levitical disciplines given as civil laws to the state of Israel apply. So why choose this one and import it into the Christian era – changing its definition by substituting a new offence – sexual unfaithfulness - in the process? The **principle** of no adultery applies, not least because it was repeated by Christ. But surely not this discipline – or any other Levitical discipline. In any case the death penalty for adultery lapsed even in the Old Testament state of Israel and was often not

---

[147] Exodus 22:16,17
[148] Although the traditional views get round this difficulty by re-defining adultery – see Appendix 4: Adultery
[149] Galatians 2:19

Appendix 2 The Levitical Death Penalty

enacted for reasons not fully understood today. [150] It was a law that was subject to change at different times, like today's death penalty in the UK that has changed over our history.

The principle

The teaching of the traditional views is wrong because it goes against a clear principle taught by Christ.

I tell you that anyone who divorces his wife, except for marital unfaithfulness, and marries another woman commits adultery. [151]

As is seen in Chapter 8 the exception – '*except for marital unfaithfulness*' - applies to the divorce and the remarriage. In other words if the divorce was for that offence, remarriage is acceptable, for both parties. The validity of the divorce is the sole factor in determining the right of the husband and wife so divorced to remarry. This is the consistent teaching of the Old Testament and is reinforced by Christ here. To forbid remarriage to a 'guilty' party based on the application of this lapsed, little understood, Levitical discipline goes against this principle.

David and Bathsheba are perhaps the most prominent example of an adulterous couple in the Bible. While they were involved in gross sins their subsequent relationship was recognised and blessed by God. From that marriage came Solomon, who is listed by Matthew in the genealogy of Christ.

It is indeed sad that the church chooses an obscure Levitical discipline to establish an erroneous point of doctrine, rather than looking to this example of grace, and seeing that the true biblical position is:-

---

[150] See Deasley 'Marriage & Divorce' Beacon Hill Press 2000 p156 where he quotes the work of CJ Wright who believes the death penalty was the maximum penalty and could be commuted to monetary compensation; also see Stephen Clark 'Putting Asunder..' Bryntirion Press 1999 pp 25,26 & 45,46. Clark believes the death penalty was only enacted when the adultery was actually witnessed.
[151] Matthew 19:9

- The Levitical death penalty was not always enacted and is in any case not a basis for establishing a Christian doctrine
- Divorce for a valid reason means freedom to remarry for both parties
- Our God is a forgiving God and does not consider adultery an unforgivable sin

But the ancient death penalty for adultery **does** reinforce the teaching that a man should not take another man's wife – and in the other marriage the husband can divorce his wife as Jesus clearly taught. The offending man's wife can divorce him based on Exodus 21 – not on something the law does not teach.

Appendix 3: Mark 10:12

If it is accepted that when Jesus makes a statement about divorce he is not necessarily giving the whole teaching on the subject - where are the other teachings found? And which ones can be considered binding today in the light of what Jesus taught? If it can be established which teachings can be assumed they can be included alongside the brief statements made in the New Testament to get a fuller picture. The church has included implied 'truths' in its own teaching on divorce for the last 500 years.

Two assumptions about the divorce passages in the gospels are found in virtually all the church's teaching. They are:-

1. The 'exceptive clause' of Matthew should be included in what Jesus said in Mark and Luke

2. Wives should be assumed to be included in the teaching about husbands and so have the same principles applied to them

It has been seen in Chapter 6 that the first assumption is a biblical and reasonable one to make. But the second assumption - that wives are included in the teaching about husbands - is not found anywhere in the Bible.

    Sometimes in the Bible the word 'man' is used in a gender neutral way that can include women. For example the Lord's statement that 'man does not live on bread alone'.[152] Jesus however throughout his teaching on divorce is talking specifically to men - to husbands, the only exception being Mark 10:12. Any view that holds that everything that Jesus says about husbands and divorce, applies to wives as well, is based on an assumption – Jesus is not recorded as teaching it.

Can this assumption be tested?

---

[152] Matthew 4:4

The Bible often contains within a statement an implied truth which can be assumed. So when Luke says:-

And everyone went to his own town to register. [153]

It can be seen from the previous verse that the 'everyone' is not the whole world but everyone in the Roman world.

Sometimes there is such a statement and common sense dictates that there is a qualification, for example Paul says:-

"Men of Ephesus, doesn't the entire world know that the city of Ephesus is the guardian of the temple of the great Artemis and of her image, which fell from heaven...[154]

Obviously it is not literally the entire world. And we say similar things. If somebody said to me – 'I would like to come and have a chat with you sometime' – and I replied 'any time!', and they turned up at 3 am – I would be surprised. Implied in my statement was any 'reasonable' time. This could be gleaned from the social context and the nature of our relationship.

Two tests

So an implied truth can often be assumed to be in a statement – but the problem is what can be implied – and when? An exegesis of any passage of Scripture needs to take the possibility of an implied truth into account, but there is a danger that no statement in the Bible can be taken at face value. I believe there are two 'tests' that can be applied which give a framework for determining the validity of an assumption.

---

[153] Luke 2:2
[154] Acts 19:35

Appendix 3: Mark 10:12

1. The hearers at the time would have fully accepted the implied teaching

This is more a guide than a test. If the beliefs of the time and the social context are understood, (no matter what the invitation said we would not normally go round to somebody's home at 3 am), it will be possible to get more quickly to a sound interpretation of a difficult verse. An otherwise obscure point can be more clearly seen. But I do not believe a doctrinal point should be built on a hidden implied truth verified by this test alone.

2. The Bible gives the teaching clearly elsewhere

This is a much more robust test. On this basis it is often reasonable to assume a hidden or implied truth in a general statement. For example Jesus said:-

But I tell you that anyone who looks at a woman lustfully has already committed adultery with her in his heart. [155]

But the Bible teaches that sexual desire for one's own wife is a good thing. [156] So an implied truth can be assumed - that this saying excludes a husband looking at his wife with sexual desire. This second test is indeed a genuine test and should be the ultimate benchmark for qualifying any plain statement in Scripture. In my view this test must be passed before a doctrinal point is made based on an assumption that a passage contains an implied truth.

In Mark 10:12 Jesus speaks for the first (and only) time from the wife's perspective:-

---

[155] Matthew 5:28 More accurately translated I believe as '..*anyone who looks at a married woman lustfully...*'
[156] For example Song of Songs and Hebrews 13:4

And if she divorces her husband and marries another man, she commits adultery.

The traditional views have largely believed to date that the Old Testament did not allow a wife to divorce her husband. So the assumption here is that Jesus introduces a new teaching that a woman could now, for the first time, divorce her husband, and the grounds – the only grounds - are the same as her husband's – that is [his] sexual infidelity. The assumption is that what is taught about husbands should be applied equally to wives. The hidden implied clause they would say is 'except for his sexual impurity'.

Those that hold to this view support their argument by saying since the penalty for adultery was death in the Old Testament, an unfaithful husband would have been executed, leaving the wife unmarried and free to remarry. Jesus was now bringing the rules 'up to date' by equalising the divorce grounds for husbands and wives. This point is considered in Appendix 2 - where it is seen to be a false analogy on several counts – not least that such a death penalty had not been enforced for many centuries.

Even if this is a correct analogy, we are still left with the problem that the hearers are to be imagined to be assuming this quite complex deduction from Jesus' short statement; he does not teach that - indeed he seems to be saying the opposite – ie **no** divorce.

So to apply the tests - does what Jesus says in Mark 10:12 really mean this:-

And if she divorces her husband and marries another man, **except only for his sexual unfaithfulness,** *she commits adultery.*

1. Would the hearers at the time have fully accepted that that was the implied teaching?
   No

2. Does the Bible give the teaching clearly elsewhere?
   No

3. Do we expect to hear this?

Appendix 3: Mark 10:12

    Yes

But this last one is not in the test!

Virtually every commentator asks of themselves that third question (probably subconsciously), provides this novel answer and proceed to expound the passage on that basis. They build their teaching about divorce on this assumption of an implied teaching that is actually nowhere in the Bible.

    This assumption actually fails the test abysmally. Nowhere else in the Scriptures Jesus' hearers are familiar with is this narrow basis for divorce by women taught, and they would be very surprised by it. His audience would not have seen this as an implied truth at all. It is a mistake to read our own world view retrospectively into the minds of Jesus' audience.

A new teaching?

Despite this hurdle most commentators say that Jesus by this teaching is giving a new rule, a 'new commandment'. Again it must be asked – is this probable? That Jesus makes a new and radical teaching by not actually saying what that teaching is, leaving us to guess what it might be. Furthermore those that hold the traditional views are in the anomalous position of believing that in Mark 10:12 Jesus is telling a woman that for the first time she **can** divorce her husband, but only on the grounds of his sexual unfaithfulness - all in a sentence that states the principle that women should **not** divorce their husbands.

    Jesus has the authority to give new teaching, and he sometimes does in pithy and enigmatic sayings. In John he tells us:-

Destroy this temple, and I will raise it again in three days. [157]

It can be learnt from elsewhere in the gospels that he was referring to his own death and resurrection. But this 'new teaching' about divorce does not appear anywhere else.

---

[157] John 2:19

What the traditional views are saying is that here is a radical new teaching, implied (not stated) in one statement, in one synoptic gospel. No serious Bible scholar would accept such an exegesis on any other subject. Wenham and Heth in 'Jesus and Divorce' take the position on the verses in Matthew that Jesus only permitted divorce **not** remarriage. They do not apply these tests to their own exegesis, but they do seem to express some discomfort with their own teaching – in that it is a radical departure from the Old Testament based on a brief gospel statement. Their own view, they concede, is not based on solid ground. But they take some comfort (somewhat bizarrely to my mind) in that the traditional views similarly rely on extracting from the brief gospel statements about husbands, where so much has to be assumed, a doctrine of divorce for wives, which also has considerable dissonance with the Old Testament. [158] And it must be remembered that this is a foundational point for the traditional views; if their exegesis of Mark 10:12 is wrong their whole teaching on divorce is fatally flawed.

If the traditional views about this are rejected, does this mean then that there is only one assumption to be made about the statements of Christ in the gospels? The assumption that the exceptive clause should be applied to all his statements about the grounds for divorce when he was speaking to husbands? Are we to really consider that the short statement in Mark 10 is the Bible's total teaching on divorce initiated by wives? But we know that is not the case. There is specific teaching about the wife's position in the Old Testament and a long history of its application. And it must be remembered that Jesus was not asked about wives, and he was not even talking about wives in the passage in Mark 10 – his comment is an aside. Is it not

---

[158] Paternoster Press 1984 See page 237.
I attempt a paraphrase of their argument here:-
Some say it is unlikely that Jesus would introduce a radical new teaching (no remarriage) in an implied statement that was contrary to the views of his audience. But to interpret these same verses to say that Jesus was allowing a woman to divorce her husband for adultery is similarly unlikely, although widely believed today. If you believe the latter (as many do) – why not the former – our equally unlikely interpretation?

Appendix 3: Mark 10:12

reasonable then to look - not to secular rationalism about gender 'equality' – but to the Bible's teaching?

It has been seen that the teaching of Exodus 21 was the widely accepted view of the day. So it would seem valid to proceed by applying the two tests that were applied to the inclusion of the husband's exceptive clause to this teaching.

The tests applied to Mark 10:12 for the implied exceptive clause 'failure to provide'

If the two tests are applied to a different assumption, a hidden clause women at the time understood to be their grounds for divorce – her husband's failure to provide - there is a quite different outcome. This is the exceptive clause for the situation where the husband has not fulfilled his duty of material and emotional support for his wife, as outlined in Exodus 21.

In other words is Jesus really saying:-

And if she divorces her husband and marries another man, **except for his failure to provide,** *she commits adultery.*

1. Would the hearers at the time have fully accepted that that was the implied teaching?
   Yes

2. Does the Bible give the teaching clearly elsewhere?
   Yes

This exceptive clause passes the tests with flying colours.

Was this teaching likely to be in the minds of the listener?

Certainly – see Chapter 6: Jesus and Divorce.

Is it taught in the Bible?

Yes it is – clearly – in Exodus 21. And Ephesians 5 repeats the husband's obligations contained in Exodus 21 and Chapter 7 shows that 1 Corinthians 7 reflects the same language in its descriptions of marital obligations. So it is with some confidence that the exception clause for wives contained in Exodus 21 can be assumed to be included in the statement Jesus made about wives in Mark 10.

Appendix 4: Adultery

The Old Testament

Adultery is a specific sin in the Old Testament – it is when a man has sexual intercourse with another man's wife. In so doing he commits adultery against that other marriage – not against his own wife. The same word is used throughout the Old Testament - and there is no doubt about its meaning.[159] The penalty was death for both the man and the woman he had been with.

Leviticus 20:10

If a man commits adultery with another man's wife--with the wife of his neighbour--both the adulterer and the adulteress must be put to death.

Deuteronomy 22:22

If a man is found sleeping with another man's wife, both the man who slept with her and the woman must die. You must purge the evil from Israel.

The penalty however was not always enforced. Adultery is specific - it is when a married woman has sexual intercourse with someone who is not her husband. In contrast sexual immorality (fornication in the King James Version of the Bible) embraces many sins – including adultery. Any sexual intercourse outside of heterosexual marriage is sexual immorality – but not necessarily adultery.

God's wisdom

Some of the laws given to ancient Israel seem strange to us but they nonetheless reveal the mind of God. If we look at the rules and punishments of Leviticus 20 and Deuteronomy 22 we see that God is doing two things:-

---

[159] *na'aph* See for example Strong's Exhaustive Concordance

Divorce and the Bible

- Protecting the integrity of family life
- Protecting the special nature of sexual intercourse

As regards family life, Leviticus 20 forbids sexual relations with family members, even those that have no blood relationship, for example step-relations and in-laws.

Adultery is all about Christ and the church

Why is the true purpose of sexual intercourse so protected in Scripture that there were such draconian punishments for any offences against God's law in this matter? Adultery, and any deviant intercourse, homosexual or with animals, was punishable by death.

Surely this is because sexual intercourse is a marriage act and that marriage act is a picture of the mystical relationship between Christ and the church. To use it in any depraved way offends God and spoils this picture of redemption. Adultery was specifically forbidden by God in the Ten Commandments - why? If a man takes another man's wife – his 'church' - the impression is given that the church can be lost – that the 'gates of Hades' might indeed overcome it despite what Jesus said. [160]

If a man has sexual intercourse with a woman who is single – neither married nor betrothed - even if **he** is married – this is not adultery. It is sexual immorality – but he is not 'stealing the church'. If the act is consensual there is not the death penalty, instead:-

If a man seduces a virgin who is not pledged to be married and sleeps with her, he must pay the bride-price, and she shall be his wife. If her father absolutely refuses to give her to him, he must still pay the bride-price for virgins. [161]

---

[160] Matthew 16:18
[161] Exodus 22:16. If the act is not consensual – in other words rape - the man has to marry her and never divorce her. Also Deuteronomy 22:28,29

Appendix 4: Adultery

Much as this might puzzle many and annoy a feminist – it is nothing to do with a patriarchal society or a disregard for women's rights. Throughout Scripture the picture of Christ and the church is protected. So while the immoral man did what was wrong – it was only the context that was wrong – he was not doing a perverted act with an animal or another man – and he was not taking another man's wife.

God is not saying it is right for a man (married or single) to have sexual intercourse with a single woman anymore than it is right for him to engage in any sexual immorality – it is simply that some sexual sins did not carry the death penalty – whereas adultery did. Many commentators are uncomfortable with this biblical discrimination, despite its exalted purpose, and either deliberately – or unwittingly – begin to blur the use of the word adultery in their own work.

The first step is often to use the word 'spouse' instead of husband or wife; this is rarely possible in an accurate exegesis of the text. It gives the impression that the terms are interchangeable, that the wife's position is the same as that of a husband. Eventually a new doctrine is slipped into the thought process – that a husband can commit adultery against his own wife. It seems so reasonable that few challenge it.

What is the significance of the point that is being made?

Once adultery is so defined, the distinctive picture embedded in the husband/wife relationship begins to fade. The equalization of the rules eventually comes to mean in the minds of many (and certainly within the Church of England[162]), that the husband and wife roles are the same. The Bible is not saying that it is alright for a husband to be sexually immoral – anymore than it is saying it is alright for him to exhibit any sinful behaviour. He is to be Christ-like to his wife. But it is saying that certain distinctives are

---

[162] As seen in Chapter 1: Marriage a Covenant. See Alternative Service Book 1980 (as amended in 2000) where the bride and groom make identical promises to each other

contained in the divorce rules that retain the picture of Christ and the church.

The traditional views re-define adultery

Most who hold the traditional views have believed that the wife had no grounds for divorce in Old Testament times. The traditional views seemed to have developed because many were sure that this 'wrong' must be righted by the gospel. But there is no such clear teaching in the New Testament. However it was clear that the Levitical death penalty for adultery would release a wife from a marriage where there had been that specific offence. So if any sexual unfaithfulness was considered to be adultery, a wife could then have her divorce grounds equalised with her husband, whose grounds for divorce are sexual unfaithfulness by the wife. Logic would demand that any 'adultery' (ie sexual unfaithfulness) by the husband in the gospel era would grant a wife a right to divorce.

The logic appears to go like this:-

- *Porneia* (sexual immorality) and *moicheia* (adultery) become interchangeable terms.

- Therefore any act of sexual unfaithfulness by the husband equates to adultery.

- In the Old Testament a man would be put to death for any act of adultery severing the marriage and freeing the wife to remarry.

- Jesus removed the death penalty for adultery by the way he dealt with the woman (ie a married woman) caught in the act of adultery as John 8 reports.

- This new dispensation of grace creates an anomaly – a wife would have to remain married to an adulterous (newly defined as sexually unfaithful) husband whereas in the Old Testament she would be free.

Appendix 4: Adultery

- This then lends weight to the interpretation that when in Mark 10:12 Jesus says a wife must **not** divorce her husband (no exceptions!) that Jesus must have really wanted the sexual unfaithfulness clause in as an exception for the wife, because this harmonises with what would have happened in the Old Testament era.

The foundation of the logic is in re-defining adultery. Much hinges on finding this new definition in the New Testament. (Quite independently of this divorce teaching many Christians are keen to see a redefinition of adultery to correct what they see as the unfair position of women.)

Several problems

- The death penalty for adultery had not existed in Israel for centuries. In any case only the occupying Romans in the New Testament era could impose the death penalty whatever the offence - which is why Christ was taken to Pontius Pilate by the Jews.

- It is to be understood that the New Testament changes the historic definition of adultery in its brief comments on the separate subject of divorce. (See below).

- It is to be accepted that the newly defined 'adultery', is to be assumed as a basis for divorce for wives, although this is never taught in the Bible.

All this is in addition to the problems outlined in Appendix 2 and Appendix 3 where it can be seen that this application of the Levitical death penalty for adultery in New Testament divorce teaching, is wrong both in application and principle. In contrast this thesis does not rely at any point on the definition of adultery changing, or staying the same. The 'correct' definition of adultery has only ever been used to support the illustration of marriage as a model of Christ and the church.

The New Testament

But does the New Testament not give the clear impression that the definition of adultery has indeed been changed there? It is possible for Christ – God in the flesh - to redefine anything he so chooses. But it must be remembered Jesus is also the word of God incarnate – and so we should be careful before we attribute to him new definitions of words that he has so carefully chosen to be preserved for us in the Old Testament – and were never the source of any doubt. Jesus lists adultery and sexual immorality separately in the same verse – indicating that they **were** different things. [163] But this of course does not necessarily mean that he was using the word adultery in the accepted way.

The easiest way to tackle this is to look at those verses where the word adultery appears to be used in an unusual way by Christ – and see what can be learned from that.

❏ Matthew 5:27,28

You have heard that it was said, 'Do not commit adultery.' But I tell you that anyone who looks at a woman lustfully has already committed adultery with her in his heart.

What is unusual here is it appears that it is possible to commit adultery without actually doing anything – and that with a 'woman' – not necessarily somebody else's wife. But there are three important points:-

1. A woman

In the Greek of the New Testament (as in contemporary French) there is no distinction between 'woman' and 'married woman'. (This is why there has been so much debate on whether women can be deacons.

---

[163] For example Mark 7:21

Appendix 4: Adultery

In 1 Timothy 3:11 when Paul says *'in the same way their wives...'* the word is *gune* and could just as well be translated *'the women'.*)

2. To lust

The Greek word translated 'lustfully' is *epithumeo* and simply means desire, with no intrinsic connotation of evil – or good. It is the same word translated 'desire' in 1 Timothy 3:1 in the King James Version and translated by NIV as *'sets his heart on'* :-

Here is a trustworthy saying: If anyone sets his heart on being an overseer, he desires a noble task.

It is the context alone that defines its nuance for good or evil.

3. The context is the Sermon on the Mount.

Jesus is teaching the spiritual nature of the 'Law and the Prophets'. And by way of illustration he takes two laws – those concerning murder and adultery. He says even if you are merely angry with your brother – that is a sin – not least because anger can lead to murder. Just because you have not murdered – do not think you are righteous. It is the heart attitude that is important. And so with adultery. Sexual desire for somebody else's wife is the starting point. That is where the sin lies – you might not have done the deed – but do not think you are righteous because of that is the point that Jesus makes.

In light of this it can now be clearly seen what Jesus is actually saying:-

You have heard that it was said, 'Do not commit adultery.' But I tell you that anyone who looks at a married woman with sexual desire has already committed adultery with her in his heart.

Our modern translators have quite validly translated sexual desire as lust – the context defining it – the context being adultery. But Jesus cannot have meant what NIV and other translations imply – that it is wrong to have sexual desire for any woman.

Paul says:-

Now to the unmarried and the widows I say: It is good for them to stay unmarried, as I am. But if they cannot control themselves, they should marry, for it is better to marry than to burn with passion. [164]

He does not say that to burn with passion is a sin – simply it is better to marry. Sexual desire for a single woman is acceptable – and surely has to be so – otherwise few men would ask for that crucial first date or want to marry! Jesus' teaching here and his use of the word adultery is entirely consistent with its Old Testament meaning.

Christ's teaching about divorce and adultery

Wenham and Heth have seen an implication in Jesus' divorce teaching that a mere (invalid) divorce is an act of adultery even without the husband's remarriage.[165] In a sense they are correct. If this seems strange – and to help understand adultery in the context of Christ's divorce teaching - consider this illustration of a legal point.

An accessory before the fact

Derek Bentley and Chris Craig were arrested in 1952 by the police after an attempted break-in to a warehouse in Croydon, Surrey. Bentley unarmed, and while being held by a police officer is alleged to have called out to his accomplice "Let him have it, Chris". After a while, Chris Craig shot and killed a police officer. Craig (age 16) was jailed; Bentley (age 19) was hanged. Bentley has subsequently been

---

[164] 1 Corinthians 7:8,9
[165] 'Jesus and Divorce' Paternoster Press 1984 p233

pardoned.

But why was it possible to charge Bentley with murder? Because in most legal systems you do not have to actually murder somebody to be charged with murder. Bentley was an *'accessory before the fact'* - that is *'one whose counsel or instigation leads another to commit a crime'*.

So the man who divorces his wife without biblical grounds leaves her in the 'legal' position of still being married. In the culture of the time she needs to remarry to live – and so her ex-husband becomes guilty of adultery – even if he doesn't remarry himself. It is not that he actually commits adultery - but rather he has become – to use the legal terminology - an 'accessory before the fact' to that offence, he has 'lead another to commit a crime'.

This legal point helps explain some of the apparent discrepancies between the gospel verses themselves (which will be looked at below), and the apparent discrepancy between the New and Old Testaments as to what constitutes an act of adultery.

❏ Matthew 5:32

But I tell you that anyone who divorces his wife, except for marital unfaithfulness, causes her to become an adulteress, and anyone who marries the divorced woman commits adultery.

This is a clear statement in line with the principle above. A man divorcing his wife without just cause would cause his wife to become an adulteress, because in the culture of the time she would probably be forced to remarry – but still technically be married to her first husband.

❏ Mark 10:11

He answered, 'Anyone who divorces his wife and marries another woman commits adultery against her.'

❏ Matthew 19:9

I tell you that anyone who divorces his wife, except

for marital unfaithfulness, and marries another woman commits adultery.

Mark 10 and Matthew 19 both record the same conversation Jesus had with the Pharisees. Here Jesus appears to say something different from Matthew 5, in that it is the man himself who would be committing adultery against his own wife if he divorces and remarries. The Mark 10:11 phrase 'against her' is not a traditional legal formula. It is found nowhere else in the Bible. [166] How is it to be translated? Mark 10:11 is the same saying in response to the same question as Matthew 19:9. As regards Matthew 19:9 there is an alternative reading that harmonises its meaning with that of Matthew 5:32 by removing any reference to remarriage. In other words it becomes….. *'and causes his wife to commit adultery'*. [167] It seems reasonable to accept the same meaning for Mark 10:11 as Matthew 5:32 and the variant reading of Matthew 19:9.

❏ Luke 16:18

Anyone who divorces his wife and marries another woman commits adultery, and the man who marries a divorced woman commits adultery.

The context of this saying of Christ is not known. As in Matthew 19 it appears the man is said to be committing adultery against his own wife when he remarries.
Raymond Collins – a Roman Catholic scholar – after some lengthy consideration of this verse believes it should be rendered:-

anyone who divorces his wife involves her in adultery, and whoever marries a divorced woman commits adultery [168]

– that Luke merely abbreviated what Christ said. This similarly

---

[166] Collins 'Divorce in the New Testament' Liturgical Press 1992 p101
[167] See John Murray 'Divorce' Presbyterian and Reformed 1961 p47,48
[168] Collins 'Divorce in the New Testament' Liturgical Press 1992 pp 179-186

Appendix 4: Adultery

harmonises the verse with Christ's statement in Matthew 5:32, and the legal perspective of being an accessory before the fact. So at first reading (the abbreviation of?) Christ's sayings recorded by the gospel writers appear to change the definition of adultery, but if the legal point outlined above is accepted it is not necessarily so.

It further helps to explain why the gospel writers did not apparently see a contradiction between themselves, or between their teaching and the Old Testament, or in the case of Matthew even within his own gospel. In any case, without this 'legal' definition of adultery, a principle of exegesis is that if there is more than one possible interpretation of a word or phrase, the one that harmonises better with the rest of Scripture should always be preferred. It seems clear that Jesus is saying the same thing in all these verses; if a man divorces his wife for no biblically valid reason she is still technically married – she is *agunah*. Any subsequent marriage by her, as clearly stated in Matthew 5:32- *'causes her to become an adulteress'*; so using the analogy above, her ex-husband is himself guilty of adultery - an 'accessory before the fact' – even if he doesn't remarry.

If it is thought that these statements by Christ about remarriage after an invalid divorce should not be so harmonised, you get the anomalous position that Jesus said significantly different things about the exact same subject, and in the case of Matthew and Mark, in answer to the same question in the same conversation. What is more it would mean that Jesus would be radically redefining a word so carefully used in the rest of the Bible. This alone should make us proceed with caution.

Also:-

- The subject of the verses is not adultery – but divorce. For a significant doctrinal point to be made we should at least have the verse address the issue – not another issue.

- Jesus has shown in the Sermon on the Mount that he can use the word adultery in a non-literal, non-legal way without changing its definition.

'Adultery of the heart' was a new concept for many.

- Jesus sometimes uses words to shock – to make a dramatic point. He says if your right hand causes you to sin – cut it off – your eye - pluck it out – without necessarily wanting us to take him literally.

There is no dispute about any of the other uses of the word adultery in the New Testament. Their context is in complete harmony with the Old Testament understanding.

Conclusion

Adultery was a specific sin hated by God for the reason given. To redefine the word on the basis of a pithy saying about divorce by Christ in the gospels is reckless, and in effect weakens the impact of the teaching of marriage and divorce and so weakens the picture God has sought to preserve from Genesis to Revelation – that of a husband and wife being a picture of Christ and the church. This thesis does not rely on the definition of adultery being consistent throughout Scripture; but the modern use of the word to indicate any marital infidelity has no clear biblical warrant. It is a concept the church has embraced to bolster its mistaken teaching that a wife should have equality; that her only grounds for divorce should be the same as for her husband. For that thesis to work the definition of the word adultery had to be changed. Even then, as has been seen, the basis of that thesis is badly flawed.

Appendix 5: Agunah

In contemporary Jewish law a marital bond is created by the two individuals – not by the rabbi – or the synagogue – or the state. Any recognition of the relationship by the state the couple reside in is a separate matter.[169] Similarly divorce is a voluntary act of the two spouses. The couple are not divorced by a decision of a court. Where a Jewish court is involved it is only in the case of irrevocable discord between the couple. Any decision by the court does not effect a divorce – it will just declare what should happen.

When a couple decide to divorce they separate and then they must give and receive from each other the *'get'* – a bill of divorce. This is a sort of 'decree absolute' that is official recognition that the marriage is over. It is the certificate that is spoken of in Deuteronomy 24. If the husband refuses to give the *get* to his wife – she is *'agunah'*. The word means although separated and to all intents and purposes divorced – she is 'bound' - or literally 'chained'. She is forbidden remarriage until she receives her *get*. She is chained to her husband until he releases her by giving her the *get.*

The outcome is that she is unable to remarry in any recognised way within the Jewish community. Children of any subsequent marriage of a Jewish woman who is *agunah* would be considered 'misbegotten' - and they would be unable to marry other Jews. But the husband is not subject to the same restrictions – even if his wife has not given him a *get*. He is able to remarry without accepting or giving the *get*. Any children of the subsequent relationship will not be 'misbegotten'.

While the outworking of this within the legislative framework of contemporary Judaism does seem manifestly unfair, it is nonetheless rooted in the biblical definition of adultery – see Appendix 4. Adultery is when a man takes another man's wife. No one would be allowed to marry

---

[169] See for the background to this the 'The Tears of the Oppressed' by Aviad Hacohen 2004 - particularly the foreword by Menachem Elott - one time Deputy President of the Supreme Court of Israel

an *agunah* woman as she was still technically married. The man could marry because in the Old Testament economy he was free to take a second wife – indeed might be commanded to do so to fulfil the responsibilities of the 'Levirate' marriage. This is where a young woman is widowed without children. Her dead husband's brother had a duty to take her as a wife (even though he might already be married) to raise up children for her. [170] Much has been written on the contemporary *agunah* problem within the Jewish communities throughout the world.

For the purposes of this thesis it can be seen that the command in Exodus 21 is to the husband to let his dissatisfied wife go free – that is 'not bound'. In effect it is a command for him to give her the *get*. Similarly in 1 Corinthians 7 Paul using similar language tells us that a believing man or woman is 'not bound' when the spouse deserts. Paul appears to be saying that the *get* can be assumed.

Agunah is a problem in the Jewish community because they have taken the legislation of Deuteronomy 24 and made their own rules based on the passage. In a Christian setting where the courts regulate divorce for a state registered marriage it is the legal system that gives the equivalent of a *get*. If for whatever reason a couple has not registered their relationship with the state it is perhaps a good idea for them to issue each other a formal 'release letter'? If they are Christians perhaps this should be done under the supervision of their church. Any such release letter should obviously not be unreasonably withheld, and I would consider that based on Exodus 21 and 1 Corinthians 7 a husband's refusal to issue such a letter would not bind an ex-wife if she had truly separated from her husband.

---

[170] Genesis 38:6-11 Deuteronomy 25:5-10 Ruth 3 & 4

Colin Hamer has been an elder at Grace Baptist Church, Astley, Manchester, England for twenty years. He is chairman of a homeless charity. He received his B.A (Hons) degree from Liverpool University in 1972. He has been married to Lois for more than thirty years and has two adult children. His first book - 'Being a Christian Husband – a biblical perspective' was published by Evangelical Press in 2005.

Reviews of 'Being a Christian Husband' included the following:

'There is a desperate need for the teaching this book gives to be made more widely known.'
Peace & Truth

'This is a well researched book exposing the way traditional gender roles in marriage have been overturned in modern times. I heartily recommend this book to all husbands and wives.'
Evangelical Times

'In a confused and confusing world a clear biblical path has been traced out for all who seek to glorify God'
Evangelicals Now

'What a needed and up-to-date book this is. It is well ordered, well written and well worth reading! I particularly found "Jesus Christ the Man" and "Jesus Christ and the Church" powerful and arresting.'
Congregational Concern

Printed in the United Kingdom
by Lightning Source UK Ltd.
116464UKS00001B/154-222